# Help, My Wife is a
# Survivor of Sexual Abuse

I am happy to provide my endorsement of Bill's book *Help, My Wife is a Survivor of Sexual Abuse*. I strongly recommend this work to those who struggle with the residual effects of childhood sexual abuse in their adult relationships, and to the mental health professionals who help them. Bill's work is exceptional for its incorporation of solid psychological theory and research along with vast clinical and client experience, as well as its notable incorporation of theological and faith issues. It is accessible, honest, and grace–filled, and sparks hope for the strength and giftedness of these couples and posttraumatic growth for both partners.

**— Noelle S. Wiersma, Ph.D.**
**Dean, College of Arts & Sciences Professor of Psychology**
**Whitworth University**

Bill's wisdom and insight has helped me navigate through the daily complexities of my wife's childhood abuse. Bill's ministry has also been key to understanding my wife's experience and how that has shaped her core perspective. This book will deeply impact how you love your survivor, while profoundly and personally changing you in the process.

**— Husband of a Childhood Sexual Abuse Survivor**

*Help, My Wife is a Survivor of Sexual Abuse* is a needed and useful resource to make sense of the roller coaster ride for men married to a sexually abused wife. The author's first–hand knowledge, vulnerability, and empathy along with psychological input provides a map to marital stability.

**— Linda Pellmann, M.A., LMFT**
**Licensed Marriage and Family Therapist, New Life Resources**

Carefully and with expertise that comes from both diligent research and painful personal experience, Bill answers the top ten questions that men married to childhood abuse survivors ask. It shouldn't surprise anyone that the longest chapter in the book is the chapter about the marriage sexual relationship! The questions he provides for personal application at the end of each chapter lead a man into a deeper understanding of himself, his spouse, and his marriage. As a pastor with abuse survivor marriages in the churches I have pastored and among people I love, I can't wait to recommend this book to them.

**— Dr. Rich Brown**
**Retired Pastor and Christian University Vice President**

# Help, My Wife is a Survivor of Sexual Abuse

Answers to Your Most Important Questions

Dr. Bill Ronzheimer

ISBN: 979-8-677-20996-3

Printed by Amazon Direct Publishing

First Printing, 2019

Marriage Reconstruction Ministries Inc.
P.O. Box 274
Circle Pines, MN 55014

www.marriagereconstructionministries.org

# DEDICATION

*This book is dedicated to Pamela, my wife.*
*You are my greatest cheerleader. Your courage, wisdom,*
*trust in God, strong and enduring faith, and deep love*
*have taught me much of what I've learned in this journey.*
*Thank you for being the love of my life forever.*

# TABLE OF CONTENTS

# FOREWORD

As a psychologist working with women and men who have been sexually abused as children, it is clear to me that the consequences of the abuse impact not only the survivor but also her or his spouse. Much has been written for those who have survived sexual abuse. Little has been available to the spouses of these survivors. I've known spouses—men and women—who have read survivor books hoping to find something to help them understand how to cope with their spouse's experience. They have also looked for explanations about what is happening in their marriage.

Actions have consequences. Abuse impacts the child, who becomes the adult, who enters into a relationship with another. Many years later that abuse has consequences for the spouse of the person abused. Just as the grown-child may not fully understand why they feel what they feel and why they act as they act, the spouse may be equally confused and hurt, unsure what to feel, unsure how to act, and often, well, lost.

*Help, My Wife is a Survivor of Sexual Abuse*, addresses needs of the spouse of the survivor.

Finally.

I've wanted this book for a long time. So many men—so many couples I've worked with—would have benefited from this book. Understanding the years-later ramifications of surviving abuse is critical to growth today. It is also critical to learn what we can do. Feelings of helplessness only contribute to the fear, shame, and often, anger. We need a map so we can find a way out of this.

Dr. Ronzheimer, Bill, makes himself available as that guide. He's been there. He knows the confusion and pain. He's walked the walk. He's lived what he's written. More than that, he's been on this journey for decades and has seen what this is about, both what is helpful and what is not. Bill has occupied many roles:

- the confused, scared, hurting, angry, husband
- the man in counseling trying to help his wife and marriage
- the overwhelmed father
- the man in counseling addressing his own needs and concerns
- the compassionate, patient, and loving husband
- the pastor

- the counselor
- the academic researcher and student
- the teacher
- the consultant
- the author

Bill shares his life, knowledge, heart, and faith to address the very real experiences and concerns that are consequences of childhood sexual abuse. He writes with the academic's concern for accuracy, the counselor's concern for relevance, and with a pastor's compassion.

Bill's growth and healing have occurred in relationship with his wife, Pamela. He has risked learning to know and be known, love and be loved with her. Today, they enjoy life's journey together as they grow and minister together.

I will recommend *Help, My Wife is a Survivor of Sexual Abuse* to spouses who seek to understand, heal, and love. I anticipate you will find it realistic and compassionate, relevant and helpful, and loving. I anticipate the fog will lift, the feelings of helplessness and discouragement will diminish, and love and hope will increase.

**— Daniel R. Green, Ph.D.**
**Psychologist, Clinical Director New Life Resources, Inc.**

# PREFACE

There is hope for you and your marriage. Bill and I have gone from a marriage filled with misery, shame, and chaos to one of hope, joy, and peace. I could not have healed so deeply had Bill not joined me in the process. As he learned what it is like to be me, Pamela, a childhood sexual abuse (CSA) survivor, I began to trust and thrive in his love.

On my first night in the hospital psychiatric ward I was so angry with God that I screamed, "God, even if you help me survive this pain, I will never let you use my pain to help or encourage another person." Suddenly every part of my life had become cruelly distorted as I relived the nightmare of my childhood sexual abuse.

How could God let a little girl endure repeated sexual abuse while He just sat there watching? Could I ever trust Him again? In that moment I was blind to the truth of God's love for me. In the weeks of that first hospitalization I slowly placed my broken fearful and wounded life in Jesus' hands. The slow process of healing had begun.

The trauma of my abuse upon our marriage was devastating and hideously unpredictable in those early months and years. I didn't realize I was projecting rage towards my abuser into our marriage. Our turmoil felt catastrophic and hopeless. Bill saw a counselor to address his own personal struggles as revealed in this book.

As the years of counseling and medication to deal with my anxiety and depression passed, our communication and intimacy grew stronger than it had been when we thought our lives were "normal." Though we are imperfect and on occasion still see areas in need of healing, Bill and I are in this journey with you as a couple. Today our marriage is a miracle of God's love and grace, God's amazing, extravagant grace.

Bill invited my input as he wrote each chapter of this book for husbands of CSA survivors. I have been the recipient of his honesty, wisdom, and tenderness in the answering of the questions most often asked. I pray that you too will find instruction and hope for yourself and your marriage. May you be rescued from despair to tell others of God's love and healing grace.

**Pamela Ronzheimer**

# ACKNOWLEDGMENTS

Our daughters, who are willing to have our story told. You loved us as parents through dark times and celebrate the times of healing. Though you too could ask many of the questions presented in this book, you always stand with us and for us as your mom and dad.

Husbands who agreed to be interviewed in my research and gave full consent to their words and perceptions being included in this work. I'm grateful for your deep desire to help other husbands. I have learned from you.

Dr. Daniel Green, your individual and couple counseling led to personal growth, and greater emotional and marital health. Your counsel and insights, often cited in this book, have made a permanent mark on my life. Thank you for your careful review of the chapters in this book, ensuring and adding to its psychological credibility.

Dr. Noelle Wiersma, your research has informed me and established for me an example of excellence. I am grateful for your support and permission to draw from constructs you generated and that I've identified in Chapter Nine.

Kirk Livingston and Tim Peterson, your friendship and professional expertise have supported and guided me in the journey towards publication. You have been quick to share helpful information and resources.

Further thanks to Kirk for doing the photo for the front cover of this book and Catherine Brinker for completing our cover design. And thanks, too, to our friend in the photo who remains anonymous.

Kirk and Tim, along with Heather Peterson, Keith Jones, Kaity Strong, and Nöelle Reuck, your editorial work went beyond grammar and included careful observation of content and how it could be most accurately stated.

The people of Alliance Bible Church in Mequon, Wisconsin, so many of you have encouraged Pamela and me, prayed for us, and supported this endeavor over a period of many years.

Dr. Basil Jackson, your challenge and encouragement for me to pursue my doctorate and your gracious and patient psychiatric counsel for Pamela was used by God to guide us through our darkest years.

Thank you to all.

# INTRODUCTION

I don't like roller coasters. How about you? Even if you are an enthusiast for wild rides, you and I can probably agree on some of its effects on riders.

For me, I don't like the steep descents because I don't like the feeling of losing my stomach. Neither do I like the long ascents that build a dreadful anticipation of the unknown ahead. I find that the unpredictable twists and turns are nerve-wracking and even irritating as I'm thrown from side to side. I don't like how some roller coasters take you through a dark tunnel, and I also don't think God designed my body to go upside-down.

When I'm on a roller coaster, my only thought is, "When will this be over?"

My wife and I have been on a rollercoaster ride; not at Six Flags, but in our marriage. My wife is a survivor of childhood sexual abuse, and if you are holding this book in your hands it's probably because your wife is a survivor as well. Or perhaps you are a survivor and you are curious about what your husband might be—or should be—reading. In either case, we know that marriages affected by a partner's childhood sexual abuse can take us into some deep descents of downward spiral that affect us in the pit of our stomach. We know the white-knuckled experience of the terrifying unknown. And like the roller coaster, our marriage has some twists and turns of the unpredictable and contradictory. One of the big questions on our minds is, "When will this emotional roller coaster be over?"

I did not know my wife was a survivor until ten years into our marriage. I was ignorant of the effects of childhood sexual abuse. At the time, that ignorance combined with my arrogance prevented us from finding the help we needed. What followed were years of emotional pain and all kinds of frustration. I'll tell you more in the chapters of this book. The simple truth is this, just like I don't like roller coaster rides, I didn't like our marriage. My wife didn't either.

There are many books that address the survivor of childhood sexual abuse and only a few that directly address husbands of survivors. If you are the husband of a childhood sexual abuse survivor, this book is for you.

"When will this be over?" is not the only question that husbands of survivors ask.

There were recurring questions that gnawed at me during the darkest years of my wife's emotional breakdown and long–term recovery from childhood sexual abuse. My doctoral research, my personal journey, and my experience as a pastor indicate that other husbands of survivors ask the same recurring questions. In this book, I have identified 10 questions that are common to husbands of childhood sexual abuse survivors.

There are four sections to each chapter in this book. First, I'll identify the question and the marital scenarios that prompt this question. Second, I will invite you to explore some potentially new perspectives that you can adopt regarding your marriage, your wife, and yourself. Third, from that new perspective, I'll recommend healthy patterns to establish in your personal and marital life. Lastly, each chapter concludes with questions for your personal consideration and application. These questions are designed to give you a starting point in helping you recognize your past and current responses to your wife while exploring new or revised approaches leading to a healthier marriage experience. However, for a more in-depth review of the chapters, we have also provided a full, free downloadable "Guide for Application" on our website www.marriagereconstructionministries.org.

As you begin, your most pressing question might be addressed in a later chapter of the book. If so, start there. Eventually, you'll want to read additional chapters as well because the other questions will eventually rise out of a deep descent or some jolting twist and turn in your marriage.

You don't need someone to talk at you with quick and easy answers. You need someone who will *walk with you* to stay on track—to find a better way. My purpose in this book is to be one of those persons for you.

Some survivors of childhood sexual abuse and their husbands wonder if there is any hope for their situation. My wife and I can understand that sense of despair. We have been in that dark tunnel of our ride.

Though we have had to do some deep soul searching within ourselves, our certainty is that the actual hope and healing comes from beyond ourselves—that God who created us has not abandoned us even though the earthly circumstances of abuse seemingly make a case against him.

I have been to theological school and have served as a pastor for four decades. But nothing has taught me more about God—His love and His presence—and about myself than this journey toward individual and marital health. This book is an invitation to join with me as we seek to stay on track in our personal and marital life.

Chapter One

# WHAT IS A NORMAL MARRIAGE?

Chad thought he and Barb had a normal marriage, not perfect but normal. Apart from her occasional complaint that he did not do enough to help keep the house clean, Chad thought she was content. He certainly was!

But it all changed 16 years into their marriage. Barb changed. She began engaging in self-destructive behaviors, had sudden outbursts of anger, went on shopping sprees spending money they didn't have, was obsessed with sexual stimulation, and wanted to escape from Chad and their daughters.

Nothing was *normal* anymore. Chad was asking himself questions he never dreamed of asking before:

*Why is she no longer interested in me?*
*Why are we always struggling and fighting?*
*Why am I being rejected?*

Quincy and Randi were in their twenty-fourth year of marriage. Randi's struggle with low self-esteem had an adverse impact on their marriage from its beginning—it was certainly having an adverse impact on Quincy. He attributed their infrequent sexual intimacy, Randi's constant struggle with her weight, and her depression and anger as by-products of her low self-esteem. Randi had been sexually abused when she was in her teens.

Quincy was tired of always reassuring Randi and felt that his emotional energy had been drained. He had nothing left to invest in their relationship. He wondered if emotional drain and relational strain were normal things in longer-term marriages or if other marriages were more tranquil.

A trusted adult had sexually abused Rob's wife Wendy for a period of several years when she was a preteen. Other people perceived Rob and Wendy to be happily married and madly in love with each other, which they were.

But Rob often wondered if other marriages had the same characteristics as his own. On the first day of their honeymoon, Wendy slept for hours as they drove to the resort where they would spend their first married days together. As Rob counted the passing mile markers and hours, he considered even more the growing distance between his *expectations* for his first day of marriage and his *experience* of it. He never expected to feel alone and for Wendy to seem so unavailable.

Three days later, Wendy told Rob that she had made a mistake getting married. She wanted to divorce. Rob reeled in emotional pain as he wondered how someone with whom he was so in love could suddenly choose to be so distant.

Little did Rob know that his first three days of marriage were offering a glimpse into the ensuing years. Wendy's extent of sleep and sometimes escape into sleep were unlike anyone that he knew. Sometimes it was impossible for him to awaken her. She lay as though comatose. On many occasions, fun activities were missed because of her sleep. While Rob would sit waiting for Wendy to awaken, he endeavored to guard his expectations but always wondered if his experience was shamefully abnormal.

What is a normal marriage anyway? In normal marriages, do wives:

- Become agitated when touched?
- Get startled at the slightest sound?
- Have routine nightmares?
- Resist kind gestures such as a bouquet of flowers?
- Burst into raging anger as suddenly as the flip of a switch?
- Injure themselves through cutting or addictive behaviors?
- Go on careless spending sprees or shoplift?
- Live in a chronic state of depression?
- Distance themselves emotionally and physically from people and even family?
- Act extremely obsessed with or totally adverse to sexual intimacy?

• Alternate between showing interest and devotion and then seeming disinterested and distant?

The alternating behaviors can be especially troubling to husbands. In general, we men think linearly. Our linear perspective leads us to function as if one set of behaviors from our wives cancels out the other. To be distant cancels out the notion and experience of interest and devotion. When the behavior alternates between contrasting behaviors, there is no "normal" to be found.

## EXPLORING A NEW PERSPECTIVE

Laura Davis, in her book *Allies in Healing*, addressed husbands of childhood sexual abuse survivors and their question of "What is normal?" Here's what she said:

> There is no such thing as a "normal" union by which to gauge your relationship. By their nature, relationships are quirky and unique, based as they are on the individual personalities and unique needs of the people involved in them.
>
> It's easy to fall into a pattern where you blame every problem in your relationship on the fact that one or both of you was abused. But the fact is that you and the survivor would be having conflicts, struggles, and rough places even if neither of you had been abused. Long–term relationships have struggles... Any two people who form a partnership are going to have to deal with differences in the way they communicate, cope with stress, and resolve conflicts; with varying levels of sexual interest, and differing needs for intimacy and independence... Although being with a survivor... adds to the complexity and intensity of these problems, you wouldn't be free of them even if both of you had the happiest childhood in the world.[1]

We can agree with Davis. People are different from one another, and so they will differ in how they relate to each other. Just about every book on marriage that I have on my shelf or nightstand describes how different we are as male and female.

Husbands and wives certainly differ in how they communicate. Picture yourself standing in a lobby filled with people. Scan the room and observe the posture that men take in conversation and how it differs from women who are in conversation. Typically, whether standing or sitting, women are positioned so that they are face-to-face, looking directly at each other as they speak. Scan the room again for two men in conversation with each other. Rather than face-to-face, they typically position themselves more shoulder-to-shoulder at about a ninety-degree angle.

I tested this one time. The guy with whom I was conversing was standing at a 90-degree angle to me. As we talked, I turned inward toward him, closing the angle. Within a few seconds, he turned outward, maintaining the 90-degree angle. I waited a moment and again turned inward toward him as we continued talking. He reciprocated by opening up that angle again. I kid you not: we completed a 360-degree circle in that conversation. If we had talked and moved faster, we would have been dancing.

Our stance in communication is different as males and females, and so is our style of communication different. I recall coming into our office suite at work one day and one of my male colleagues was feeling grumpy. He was annoyed with a certain situation. Rather than soothe him, I goaded him for his grumpiness. We both laughed in our understanding of each other. Having overheard our bashing and bantering, a female staff member came out of her office and said, "I wish women could talk like that and then laugh. If women spoke like that to each other, they'd be offended and wouldn't be able to speak to each other for weeks."

When male/female differences are brought into marriage, it gets messy. It's complicated! Jeff and Shaunti Feldhahn bring to life the differences between men and women in their companion books *For Men Only* and *For Women Only*. They state, "Women's thought lives are like busy computers with multiple windows open and running all at once."[2] These open windows include thoughts and emotions from the past and present, all at the same time. One of the differences is that "women seem consistently unable to close these windows as easily as men can."[3]

It's no wonder then that a guy might protest, "Why does the past keep coming up?" It's because past and present merge in the thought processing for women. It's also no wonder why an argument might get settled and a few minutes later the guy wants to have sexual intimacy with his wife. For him, the window on the argument closed. Perhaps his computer—thinking—even shut down.

And what about all the variations in personality? Some people, my wife is one of them, love going back to the same restaurant and they typically order the same thing. Likewise, some return to the same vacation spots. The sameness makes perfect sense to them. Why take a chance when you can go with the known and proven? The sameness offers comfort and security.

Others seek adventure. They love trying the new restaurants and vacation spots. They too, can be very rational in their approach as they seek to avoid boredom. But even among these adventurers, the differences are obvious. For some, the adventure is found in discovering new camping sites and hiking expeditions while others find the adventure in downtown clubs, concerts, and museums. Given such diversity, how would we ever define or describe "normal?"

No two individuals are completely alike. Put any two individuals together and you discover that the variables among couples will be even greater.

Is all of this true of every individual male and every individual female? No. But that just builds the case further of how different we are—each of us is unique. If you don't like being put into a category of a certain group, it merely speaks to the point that we are markedly different from one another.

Davis made a good point. There's too much quirkiness, too much uniqueness, and too much circumstantial unpredictability (e.g., job loss, illness, promotions, death, mobility, etc.) from which to expect a norm. As noted by Milan and Kay Yerkovich in *How We Love*, "'Normal' is just a setting on a dryer."[4]

Nevertheless, as Davis acknowledges, the effects of childhood sexual abuse can intensify the challenges of marriage.

Wes's wife, Jyl, got really mad at him when he tried to help her out by changing the diaper of their daughter. It wasn't that he was doing it wrong. It was that he was doing it at all that enraged her. Most of us guys would be thinking, "Holy cow! What wife objects to her husband helping out by changing a diaper? That's unconditional love!!!" Wes could argue that many wives would normally view his act of kindness with favor rather than anger.

Wes also wondered why, after having sexual intercourse, Jyl expected special attention and even gifts for the next few days. It was as though she wanted to be rewarded for being special to him. Was that a normal thing in marriage?

Eventually, Wes learned that Jyl's father would give her special treatment during the days subsequent to sexually abusing her at night. He was also able to assume that his kind intention in changing their daughter's diaper was viewed by Jyl with suspicion, not because of what Wes was doing, but because of what her father had done.

Wes believed that a marriage affected by childhood sexual abuse has "more things to work through than in a normal relationship." Wes's counsel to men preparing to marry a survivor of childhood sexual abuse was that "you have to be ready for all sorts of things that would not come up in a normal relationship."

And what about husbands whose wives have a suicidal ideation because of their childhood sexual abuse? There were times I came home and did not know if I would find my wife in the garage with the car running. It was terrifying! I was overwhelmed with fear and confusion.

*How could I bear the loss of her?*
*How would I tell our daughters?*
*What would I do with the happy memories?*
*What could I have done to soothe her tormented mind?*

I knew that most of my guy friends were not dealing with these kinds of questions and this level of trauma.

Laura Davis made a noteworthy observation. If there is anything normal to marriage, it is the ongoing relational adjustments to our individual quirkiness. Not every quirk is attributable to the childhood sexual abuse inflicted on our wives. Nevertheless, the abuse does bring unique and sometimes traumatic dimensions into the marriage. What happens then?

## ESTABLISHING NEW PATTERNS

I sat one day in my counselor's office grumbling about how I wanted a normal marriage. He asked me, "What's normal?" I had enough sense to refrain from answering his question; I would have only embarrassed myself.

But since you and I don't have to say anything out loud right now, "let's give it a go" as they say in the U.K. "What do we mean by a normal marriage?"

Stop reading for a moment and give that question some thought. Then come back to read further.

What do we mean by "normal marriage?" What are we really referring to? Are we referring to someone else's marriage? Are we thinking of our parents' marriage?

How do you answer and what does it reveal about you?

I know there were times when I thought my marriage should be more like my parents' marriage. Yikes! Do I really want my wife to be like my mom? Yet, that's how many husbands feel and function.

It is a common phenomenon for a man to want his wife to be like his mom. A mother is the first important woman in a man's life. Our mothers comfort us. They "teach" us about women. Therefore, a husband can naturally relate to his wife not as the man he is but as the boy he was. It can even seem normal.

But why should my wife forfeit her uniqueness? And why should yours? Whom of us husbands do well when we are expected to be like someone else?

Another manner by which we might describe normalcy in marriage is in terms of a guy at work or church who seems to have a normal marriage. Why do you think that? What makes you think you know what their marriage is really like? I don't mean to inflict judgment that all other marriages are undesirable, but I do know that no marriage is without disagreement, bad breath, facial hair, poorly timed statements, and matters that are kept private.

Many couples experience years of marriage before the effects of their childhood sexual abuse become intrusive on their union and lifestyle. Sometimes it is because of delayed disclosure and sometimes it is because of the latent nature for some effects of childhood sexual abuse.

Therefore, some husbands of survivors describe their marriage as having been normal in the months/years before dealing with the effects of the abuse. That's what I thought for several years. I thought I had a normal marriage for the first ten years. My wife and I had normal children, normal celebrations, normal habits, normal communication, normal sex, and normal arguments.

But after a series of sessions with a counselor, we discovered various dysfunctional patterns that existed during the years that we thought were "normal." For example, when we entered into marriage, one of the long-term effects of my wife's childhood sexual abuse was that she had been silenced. She was not silent in the sense of being a wallflower. She was expressive and fun-loving, the person you wanted at your party. But she was silent when it came to being opposing or objecting. As a result, she did not verbalize any objection to my manner of domination. Her dysfunctional silence led me to believe that she was compliantly content with my dysfunctional dominance of which I was unaware.

**We discovered various dysfunctional patterns**
**that existed during the years**
**that we thought we were "normal."**

My father, as many dads of his generation, was manager of our home. Mom's life and identity were wrapped up in him. I don't remember her ever disagreeing with him, at least not in front of us kids. Those who knew my dad viewed him as gentle and kind. It's not that he wasn't kind, but he was king. And as king, he was always right in the eyes of the family. And though he was not physically or verbally severe, it was clear that he was to be served.

I definitely benefited from how my dad made sure that my siblings and I learned spiritual truths and had opportunity to serve God. And he was a tremendous provider of our physical needs. But I was not aware of the relational subtleties and deficiencies in our home. In my ignorance, I became a *carrier* of the relational dysfunctions into my adulthood.

I mirrored my dad as I entered the early years of our marriage with the assumption that I was right and my wife was to agree. I held control, and she was to be content. I made the decisions, and she made no objection, out loud that is. Her being silenced made us a perfect match. No! Her being silenced made us a perfectly dysfunctional match.

Since she was silent, I considered her to be in agreement. In fact, I thought her to be thrilled over my control. And since she had been controlled in the earlier years of her abuse—as is any survivor—one of the long–term effects for her was to subconsciously accept that framework of control.

As my wife gained mental and emotional health through her counseling, the residual powerlessness that was an effect from her abuse was exchanged for a new sense of efficacy (worth, value, and ability). She did not seek to be domineering, but she did seek to be in control of her wellbeing. As a result, when I placed my wellbeing over her wellbeing, she spoke.

Fortunately, I was getting some beneficial counseling as well. For one thing, I was learning that what I thought was normal was not necessarily best. As a caring counselor listened and responded to my tirades and tears, I began to understand for the first time in my life what it was like to be on the other side of me.

I am grateful for the counseling I received. I benefited from the wise counsel of a psychologist who enlightened me and exposed my dysfunctional and egotistical patterns. But I also needed God who empowered me to experience the needed transformation.

As I confessed my pride and presumption, God began building in me a new understanding of what it is to love. I began understanding that to love my wife was to honor her.

As I grew in love and my wife grew in emotional well–being, our marriage was transformed. We discovered unity, satisfaction, contentment, the thrill of growing together, and the joy of being knit together. Consequently, **neither one of us wanted to go back to our earlier years when I thought things were normal.**

Here's what I've concluded:

*It is preposterous to seek a normal marriage.*
*It is prosperous to strive for a healthy marriage.*

Striving for a healthy marriage begins with you. The aim of this book is to guide husbands in developing healthy perspectives and patterns, and that development begins with self–awareness. This self–awareness and the development of new perspectives and patterns do not occur overnight. Your patience will be tested. Furthermore, the journey will take you outside of your comfort zone.

Some men are looking for easier answers. Their norm is "Just tell me what to do!" But before you put this book down, consider this: the journey I'm talking about is one of development. The current journey most husbands are on is a journey of destruction. It's your awareness of pending destruction and persistent despair that prompted you to begin reading this book. So, don't stop now.

Is endurance necessary? Yes. Is enduring love necessary? Yes. Will you feel like you are going backwards at times? Certainly!

You will have a sense of "three steps forward one step back." But that experience goes with any development. Have you ever tried to develop your golf swing? It's not an overnight process and there are times you are tempted to quit, at least for a while. But most people are willing to pay the price of time, effort, and endurance.

**It is preposterous to seek a normal marriage.**
**It is prosperous to strive for a healthy marriage.**

When you are on the path of personal and marital development, the gain begins to outweigh the pain; your enriched life begins to diminish your enraged strife.

So how do we gain self–awareness and develop new perspectives and patterns? Here are some initial steps that, in my experience, have contributed to personal health and welfare. These initial steps are not intended to be a comprehensive outline. More will be unfolded throughout the chapters of this book.

### 1. Draw Lines Of Responsibility

Husbands of childhood sexual abuse survivors are vulnerable to feeling as though their wife's stuff is because of what they as husbands have done or have not done. This is especially true when husbands are the recipient of their wife's inner rage or outer distancing.

Dan's wife, Nikki, kept him at arms–length because she did not fully trust him. Some wives have good reason not to trust their husband. But Dan had been faithful to Nikki and had proved himself trustworthy. Yet, their relationship conflict was often due to Nikki's mistrust of him. Dan's protest was captured in these words: "It was just frustrating. I can't climb this dang mountain fast enough or high enough to get over whatever imaginary barrier Nikki set and damn it, I'm ready to be done with it."

My counselor, Dr. Daniel Green, spoke to me of the importance of a clear understanding of personal responsibilities and responsibility boundaries. "I am responsible for how I treat myself and how I treat others. I am not responsible for how others treat me, treat each other, or treat themselves."[5] Therefore, my emotional health and personal sense of well-being means setting boundaries of responsibility, knowing that I am not responsible for my wife's childhood sexual abuse or for her response to it.

I must embrace that for which I am responsible and release what is her responsibility. In so doing, she is empowered, and I am freed.

## 2. Don't Bury Or Deny Your Emotions

From childhood, most of us guys have been taught the same thing. The verbal instruction may have varied—"Buck up!" "Don't cry!" "Be a man!" But the lesson was always the same: "Don't feel!" So, we do all we can to stuff our feelings.

But emotions—I am using emotions and feelings interchangeably—cannot be buried, denied, or avoided. They are very real and unavoidable. One husband I've interviewed said, "I have a temper, but I'm not angry." His denial avoided the truth that his temper revealed his anger. Our blood pressure, heart rate, and muscle tension are linked to our emotions. So is our behavior.

Green and Pope list and define ten basic emotions:

1. *Happiness, Joy*: These are feelings that prompt a continued course of action .
2. *Acceptance, Trust*: These are feelings of affiliation and safety.
3. *Anticipation*: These feelings occur when we are motivated to explore or pursue a situation.
4. *Surprise*: These feelings accompany the discovery of something new and/or unexpected.
5. *Anger*: The feeling that something is wrong and not the way it ought to be.

6. *Hurt*: This feeling accompanies being harmed or abused.

7. *Sadness*: Feelings of loss.

8. *Fear*: This feeling accompanies awareness of danger.

9. *Disgust*: The feeling that accompanies our desire to turn away from a scene or situation.

10. *Shame*: A feeling of disconnection, numbness, wishing to hide.[6]

I often hear other husbands say the exact words that I've said, "I'm frustrated" or "I get frustrated when…" I've even said, "I'm not angry. I'm just frustrated." Typically, that statement is a denial of anger because frustration is a combination "of these basic emotional states. For example, frustration may be experienced with a combination of anger and fear, or it may be a combination of anger and sadness and hurt."[7]

The first step to not burying our emotions is to be **aware** of them. In other words, I need to be honest with myself regarding the feelings that reside within me. Why? Because they have power! My feelings, and yours, influence our physiological and behavioral reactions.

Second, I need to **admit** my feelings. This can be problematic.

Husbands of survivors sometimes stuff their feelings of anger because they fear (feeling) the response from their wives if their anger were to be admitted. The challenge for their wives is that, as survivors of childhood sexual abuse, they already feel unworthy of anyone's love and favor. So, when a husband admits his feelings of anger, his wife might interpret it as, "You *are* angry with me. I knew it! I knew you didn't love me! You can't love me."

Husbands of survivors can also experience shame. Perhaps you've attended a men's conference at your church and one of the topics on the schedule for the day is "Sexual Intimacy in Marriage." You try to figure out how to get out of that session because you're embarrassed by the fact that, for you, sexual intimacy seems to occur as frequently as the Bears winning the Super Bowl. The perversion of sexuality that heaped shame on your wife has resulted in an infrequency of intimacy that heaps shame (feeling of disconnection) on you.

Feelings like anger and shame can be quite parasitical to our soul and to our body. I must be aware of them, and I need to admit them.

Here's another principle I learned from Dr. Daniel Green: *If you name it, you tame it.* First, we need to name it to ourselves. Dig out the feeling and bring it to the surface before it digs further into us. It's best when we can then name it to someone else, preferably a counselor, pastor, mentor, or trusted friend. The flammable nature of the feeling can be extinguished or significantly diminished when we say our feelings rather than stuffing our feelings.

The day can come for you to admit your feelings to your wife. Your timing and motive will be key factors for a healthy outcome. Hopefully, your feelings will be tamed so that you are not *backing up your truck and dumping everything* on your wife just to get it off your mind. This is why you need a trusted friend or counselor. Dump your toxic stuff on them. When you speak with your wife, your goal is to be sensitive to her shame, pain, and needs while being vulnerable about your own shame, pain, and needs.

**When you speak with your wife, your goal is to be sensitive to her shame, pain, and needs while being vulnerable about your own shame, pain, and needs.**

### 3. Self-Care

What do you enjoy doing? What activity brings a feeling of "I'm glad I did that!" when it is completed? Some husbands of survivors have been addressing the needs of their wives for so long, that they cannot remember the last time they just relaxed and had some fun.

So, what do you enjoy doing and when is the last time you've done it?

Here's a list of possible stress relievers:

- Golf (not on my personal list)
- Fishing (Nope! Not that either)
- Hiking
- Motorcycling
- Cards
- Reading
- Community recreational leagues
- Movies
- Skeet shooting
- Cooking
- Photography

- Model building
- Woodworking
- Going to a sports event

Begin now. Decide on what you need to do and develop your plan for engaging in healthy self-care activity on a regular basis that will offer fun and replenishment. Communicate your needs and ideas to your wife so that she is not suddenly wondering what you are up to. It is necessary for your own individual growth and the health of your marriage that you express and address your own needs.

For some of you, I know that expressing your needs like this to your wife is an intimidating idea. From my conversations with husbands, I know that some of you might hear, "What? You are concerned about your needs? So tell me, how have you suffered?" I'm sure it must be tough to receive a response like that. If that happens to you, it's time to go back and draw lines of responsibility.

Being faithful in your marriage does not mean being negligent to your own needs that come with being human. Self-care means regularly engaging in activities that are appropriate morally, healthy physically, and rejuvenating emotionally. Do what you love to do.

> **Self-care means regularly engaging in activities that are appropriate morally, healthy physically, and rejuvenating emotionally.**

Self-care may also mean that the healthy thing for you is to get counseling for yourself. Self-care recognizes our personal coping limitations and willingly seeks out a counselor who can be our competent confidant.

Here are a few tips that can be helpful in finding a good counselor:

- Talk to your pastor and ask for his recommendations.
- Go online and check out the core beliefs and values of the counselor or counseling center.
- Do you sense the counselor understands you?
- Expect that the counselor will ask thought-provoking questions of you.

• Don't expect your counselor to concentrate on your wife (because she is not there in the session).

Accept the fact that the counseling will involve more sessions than you may initially anticipate. You are seeking counsel because you want a qualified counselor's insights into matters that you initially do not or cannot perceive. The process and truth being sought requires time to unravel complex issues and create new patterns.


## CONCLUSION

As I sit here entering my thoughts into my laptop, I wonder about who I would describe as being "normal." I also wonder if I am doing any of my friends and acquaintances a favor if I were to designate them as "normal."

Do I want to be described as "normal?" I don't think I want to be described as "abnormal," but what does it mean anyway to be described as "normal?" Normal compared to what? Normal based on whose standards? Normal according to whose perspective?

What does it really mean if anyone is described as being normal? What does it really mean if a marriage is described as being normal?

There are two concepts important for individual and marital health: uniqueness and intimacy.

You and I may have similarities; perhaps similar hobbies, likes and dislikes, sense of humor, spiritual beliefs, or level of education. But even if you and I were similar in all of these areas, we are profoundly unique.

You and I share the incredible quality that we have been made in the image of God; each of us has the capacity for socialization, decision-making, and thought. Nevertheless, we are unique—that's how God made us. He is imaginatively and ingeniously creative. My life honors God's incredible creativity as I live according to my uniqueness rather than attempting to be like someone else. My emotional health is determined, in a large part, by my refusal to live as though I were someone else and resolve to live in keeping with how God uniquely shaped my personality and giftedness.

Individual uniqueness results in marital uniqueness. No husband and wife can ever duplicate the marriage of another man and woman. Therefore, any comparison of our marriage to any other's marriage is foolishness. The health of your marriage and mine is determined by our refusal to live as though we were some other couple and resolve to live according to the uniqueness that we and our wives bring to our own marriages.

Intimacy, important to marital health, is knowing my wife and being known by my wife. Knowing includes exploring her thoughts and feelings; understanding the thoughts, feelings, and experiences that lie behind her actions, reactions, and responses. Our knowing ranges from discovering all that she reveals about her past and exploring all that she anticipates for her future. Intimacy increases as we observe and absorb the significance of her words, gestures, facial expressions, posture, and movement.

Likewise, and of equal importance to this intimacy, is how I allow myself to be known. Being known includes openly and freely sharing my thoughts, feelings, experiences, past pains and pleasures, and future hopes and fears. Being known is fostered by pouring myself out to her rather than her having to probe as though prying open a rusty old can.

Intimacy is enriched and enduring because of the unique quality of our wives and ourselves. God has something better for us than "normal." God's design for our marriage is two unique people, knowing and being known through truth and love.

**God's design for our marriage is two unique people knowing and being known in truth and love.**

## Chapter One: Personal Application

1. What does your description of normal marriage reveal about you?

2. What have you been taught, verbally or nonverbally, about emotions from your childhood?

3. What are three steps you can take this week to know your wife more deeply? For example, what questions can you ask? What gestures do you observe and how do they inform you about your wife?

4. What steps can you take this week to be known? For example, how will you tell your wife about your day and then also inform her about your responses to your day?

For a more in-depth review of this chapter, we have also provided a full, free downloadable "Guide for Application" on our website: www.marriagereconstructionministries.org.
It is our hope that the additional questions in this guide will take you further into potential personal and marital growth.

Chapter Two

# WHEN DO I GET MY WIFE BACK?

Wes and Jyl were in their late 50's and had been married for 36 years. It wasn't until their 33rd year of marriage that Jyl disclosed her childhood sexual abuse. They had experienced over 30 years of marriage without any conversation, contentiousness, or counseling that focused on the known effects of childhood sexual abuse. But now, since the disclosure, both of their lives were consumed with the abuse's effects.

Jyl's abuse began when she was 3 years old and it continued on a frequent basis for 10 years. Her father was the perpetrator, which intensified the wreckage and complicated her recovery. Her effects included depression and dissociation. When I first met Wes, I admired his sincerity, compassion, and commitment to Jyl's healing. But the process of Jyl's healing was also testing his patience. He seemed to be experiencing some compassion fatigue. A year and a half into Jyl's counseling, Wes went to visit her counselor believing that after 18 months of counseling, things ought to be better. He made sure the counselor understood his expectations and then asked, "When do I get my wife back?" Wes felt he had lost the wife he knew for over 30 years. Chad and Barb had been married for 36 years when I first met Chad. In the early years of their marriage, Chad and Barb shared common values and convictions. They were very active in their church and their lifestyle was conservative by most people's standards. From Chad's perspective, he had a great marriage, great family, and great life.

But sixteen years into their marriage, Barb became a different woman. She made some lifestyle changes that Chad found horribly disturbing. Barb's changes included choices that were contradictory to the strong religious beliefs she had held all her life. She stopped attending church, began smoking, and went bar–hopping with friends. In private, her sexual indulgence was described by Chad as "bizarre." She showed no interest in Chad, wanted to leave the marriage and their two daughters, and frequently contemplated ending it all by ending her life.

Chad's bewilderment and question about when he would get his wife back was conveyed in the form of a statement. He said, "I didn't want to lose her… I wanted the former woman I married."

My wife disclosed her childhood sexual abuse ten years into our marriage. My failure to respond empathetically and proactively delayed her receiving the help she needed. As a result, she experienced a complete emotional and physical breakdown eight years later and was admitted into inpatient psychiatric care for four weeks.

The year of her breakdown became the pivotal year in our lives. Events are still recalled and categorized by whether they occurred in the pre–breakdown–years or post–breakdown–years. Even though there were major ups–and–downs that followed the breakdown year, nothing marked our lives or time as much as that year.

I often longed to return to the marriage we had during the pre–breakdown years. I wanted to get the wife back that I knew during those eighteen years even though I had not treated her as respectfully as she deserved during that time.

It is as though marriages involving a survivor of childhood sexual abuse can have an Act I and Act II. Husbands in Act II long for the wife they had in Act I. There are at least three explanations for this two–act experience.

**It is as though marriages involving a survivor of childhood sexual abuse can have an Act I and Act II.**

### 1. The Initial Or Additional Disclosure Of Abuse Can Be A Turning Point

While disclosures are the communication of the bad news of the abuse, the act of disclosure itself is good news for two reasons. First, if you are the one hearing the disclosure, the survivor considers you to be a person of safety for disclosing what seems to be so shameful for them. A sense of safety is the prerequisite for a survivor to disclose their abuse. Secondly, the disclosure indicates that the survivor has gained enough insight to link a current situation with the past violation. They are facing the reality of the abuse in spite of its incomprehensible ugliness.

A variety of events can trigger a survivor's suppressed or forbidden memories of the childhood sexual abuse they endured. The recall that is triggered can lead to either an initial disclosure or fuller disclosure.

A short list of seemingly endless possibilities for triggers includes:

• The content of a news report
• A comment on social media
• A survivor's child reaches the age they were when the abuse occurred
• Individuals in addiction recovery can have memories triggered when the drug or alcohol is no longer suppressing their memoires
• Visiting a location from childhood
• Bathing
• The death of the perpetrator
• A change in body chemistry
• Sights, smells, and sounds associated with the abuse

The initial or fuller disclosure of childhood sexual abuse can indicate that the survivor is contending with or seeking to cope with its effects. Perhaps the cumulative nature of the effects is taking its toll on the survivor or the effects are intensifying in their level of frequency or depth of intrusion. Either of these possibilities points to an interference with the daily life and routine of the individual and the couple.

**The initial or fuller disclosure of childhood sexual abuse can indicate that the survivor is contending with or seeking to cope with its effects.**

Like Wes, Chad, and me, some husbands enter into marriage without knowledge of their wife's childhood sexual abuse. These husbands might experience an *Act I* for years before their wife discloses her abuse. Her disclosure often marks the turning point in the relationship.

In other situations, husbands enter their marriage knowing that their wife had been sexually abused as a child yet do not know the full extent of the abuse or the impact of its effects. Years later, these couples can experience a turning point in their marriage when the effects of the wife's childhood sexual abuse invade and interfere with their relationship and the established routines of Act I. This turning point might be accompanied by a fuller disclosure of the abuse.

For some couples, the effects can intensify and interfere yet without disclosure; the memory of the abuse is deeply lodged in the recesses of the survivor's memory. As the inner conflict mounts in the survivor, the tension and conflict in the relationship also mounts. Even with no disclosure, a husband might be able to identify a circumstance or phase when *everything* seemed to change.

### 2. The Latent Nature Of Some Effects

The second explanation for the two–act experience in marriage is that some of the effects of childhood sexual abuse can exist in a latent state. It might be months or years into the marriage before these effects manifest themselves.

Vince and Julie entered their marriage with the usual arguments that occur with marital adjustments. It seemed that they had sufficient conflict resolution skills and sought ways to continue developing those skills. Julie was a peacekeeper, so there were never any knock–down–drag–out fights.

Julie had grown up in a large family that was conflicted. As the oldest, she took on the self–appointed responsibility of keeping peace and she carried that attribute into marriage. Vince assumed all was well and that Julie was happy in life and with him. And for the most part, Julie thought she was happy in life and with Vince.

But more than 15 years into their marriage, Julie could no longer keep the lid on the underlying anger and rage that were rooted in the childhood sexual abuse which had occurred when she was age 10. There were times when Julie suffered from poor choices that Vince had made—choices that undermined Julie. Her expression of anger on those occasions was to be expected. But there were other times when, in her words, "she just lost it."

Julie's biggest outbursts of anger came when she felt that she was not being understood in the moment. Her outbursts never occurred with others; they were only with Vince. She would go on the attack. Vince felt he was put on trial, and the prosecuting attorney, Julie, was unleashing condemning questions and surprising accusations in such rapid succession that he could not begin to form a thought, much less an answer.

Julie's desperate desire to connect and be understood by Vince resulted in disconnection with Vince. Vince wanted the peacekeeper he had known in Act I of their marriage and wished she would return.

Julie's outrage and cry for understanding had deep roots. As a ten–year–old, she stood accused by her schoolteachers for being in areas of the school building that were off limits to her. But it was the place her perpetrator, one of the teachers, took her in order to inflict sexual abuse upon her. As Julie stood accused, the seed of outrage for not being understood was planted. Yet it would be decades before that outrage burst forth into full bloom. It was a latent effect of her abuse.

### 3. False Assumptions

The third explanation for the two–act marriage experience is the false assumption that the effects of childhood sexual abuse will be inconsequential. Some men notice the effects during their dating relationship but dismiss them, either viewing them inconsequential or as something that can be conquered. I've met husbands in their 20's who acknowledged that their wives were sexually abused but who claimed that it was not affecting their marital relationship. In some of those situations, I've been able to hear their wives' more accurate perspective at a subsequent time. While the effect may not have been outwardly manifested enough at the time to appear consequential, it inwardly rumbled in the survivor as hot lava waiting to erupt.

Dan and Nikki each had their own previous dating relationships that included sexual promiscuity. When they began their relationship together, they committed themselves to build their relationship on the firmer foundation of spiritual, social, and emotional intimacy and save the sexual intimacy for marriage. As they explored their inner qualities, Nikki disclosed the sexual abuse of her childhood. They talked it through between themselves and with others. As their wedding approached, they had proven faithful to their goals and to one another. The healthy foundation of love and respect had been built.

As they got to their hotel room on their wedding night, at the appropriate time, Dan began unzipping Nikki's dress. Tears filled and flowed from Nikki's eyes, but not from being overwhelmed with joy and gratitude. Instead, Nikki's past invaded her present. Fear and shame sabotaged all that she and Dan had anticipated.

Nothing that touches the depth of our personhood—nothing that happens to us sexually—is inconsequential. As much as we men might hope to compartmentalize unfavorable experiences into corners of our lives and relationships, we are nevertheless "intricately made and woven together (Psalm 139)."

The cumulative effects and increasing intensity of the effects take their toll on the survivor, the husband, and the marriage. Husbands recall earlier years of more youthful resilience and less marital resistance. The effects of abuse intrusively interfere with all of the desires and dreams of both husband and survivor. For the husband, he wonders when he will get his wife back.

> **Husbands recall earlier years of more youthful resilience and less marital resistance.**

### EXPLORING A NEW PERSPECTIVE

A new perspective begins with identifying loss that has occurred in the relationship. After identifying the loss, understanding the ambiguous nature of the loss can bring insight to a husband's anxiety over that loss.

### 1. Identify The Loss

Loss lies at the core of wondering when you will get your wife back. Your sense of loss can include loss of the familiar, loss of your perception of "normal," loss of what you perceived as a more carefree time in your marriage, loss of the person that you thought you married, and loss of the life you anticipated.

The sense of loss is prevalent among men whose wives are survivors of childhood sexual abuse.[8] It permeates the marriage relationship, exists as a continual underlying disturbance, and is experienced at multiple levels. Consider the following possibilities of loss.

## A. *Loss Of Emotional Connection*

Some husbands experience the loss of emotional connection with their wives. This loss can be intensified when their wives begin to process the trauma of the abuse. The survivor's emotional energy is invested in working through the trauma and simply trying to survive from day to day. For a husband, the survivor seems distant. Husbands often verbalize this loss as "She's just not there."

The loss of emotional connection can also be due to the survivor's anger towards her perpetrator, which sometimes gets directed toward her husband. In this case, a husband feels emotionally "stiff-armed" by his wife. If this is your experience, then it is a time to remember again that your *wife's response to you may affect you, but it is not about you.*[9]

The emotional distance can also include physical distance. Survivors can experience an urge to escape. Their inability to find an escape when they were being abused in the past can emerge in the form of actual escape in the present.

Some of the most painful times I've encountered were the occasions when my wife took an escape route in her anxiety and anger over her abuse. These occasions were sudden and terrifying. The triggers that led to her anger and escape usually came out of our conversations. Tensions escalated, reason evaporated, and escape was executed. There was no stopping her as she grabbed the keys to her car. Only my physical force—which I would not exert—could have stopped her, maybe. On one occasion, I remember looking out our bedroom window and seeing her racing in the wrong direction down the boulevard in front of our home. I felt intense terror then and still can feel the fright as I recall the scene now. I also felt totally alone in this world. Who could I ever confide in? I never called the police but sometimes called her doctor. And I prayed. Only God could keep her safe, and He did. Hours later, she returned, exhausted and unsettled.

Today, as we review those terrifying flights from years ago, we both know that the escapes were the behavior of the 9-year-old, sweet, and innocent girl who wanted to get away from her perpetrator, tried to get away, but could not get away. Thinking back to her evening escapes, she now teaches, "all the feelings of those moments were the terror that the 9-year-old girl felt."

A survivor's suicidal ideation can be an additional contributor to emotional disconnect. For Chad, not only did Barb want to leave the marriage and their daughters, she wanted to kill herself. The absence of any desire for connection on the part of the survivor strikes at the core of a husband. The emotional disconnect is intensified by his fear of actual disconnect.

> **The survivor's inability to find an escape when she was being abused in the past can emerge in the form of actual escape in the present.**

Shame is the unintended consequence for the husband of the emotional disconnect that occurs in our marital relationship. This shame is an inner torment. Shame does not necessarily come from something I've done. It can come from how someone else is treating me.

Kaufman stated, "To live in shame is to feel alienated and defeated, never quite good enough to belong. And, secretly, we feel we are to blame, that the deficiency lives with ourselves, alone."[10] Therefore, husbands experiencing an emotional disconnect from their wife experience loneliness, inner torment, the sense of rejection, and the gnawing feeling that they are deficient and wrong.

Consequently, when emotional disconnect occurs, a husband is inclined to ask, "What did I do wrong?" The answer to that question is often, "Nothing! You are experiencing the pain of the disconnect." Trying harder does not forge a reconnect. Neither does blame.

As husbands, we must keep in mind that our wives are experiencing much of the same despair even though, to us, it may seem that our wives are imposing all the negativity upon us. Wives, as survivors, are also experiencing self–rejection, that casts them into a pit of isolation, despair, and self–blame.

> **… our wives are experiencing much of the same despair even though, to us, it may seem that our wives are imposing all the negativity upon us.**

## B. Loss Of Productivity In Daily Functions

Survivors of childhood sexual abuse develop coping mechanisms to override the pain of their trauma. For some survivors, the quest for achievement serves as their coping mechanism. When they marry, their husbands cheer them on to further accomplishments.

But years later, the coping mechanisms can no longer drown the pain of trauma. The energy that had been expended in performance and accomplishments becomes redirected towards survival. The completion of projects is delayed, chores are ignored, appointments are missed, phone calls are not returned, and excuses are made. The shift in productivity leaves a husband wondering what happened to the capable woman he married.

## C. Loss Of Sexual Intimacy

Survivors who have not yet been counseled through the damaging effects of childhood sexual abuse enter marriage with distorted notions about sexuality. They've been conditioned from the abuse to think that the sexual relation is about "servicing" another person. In marriage, she views sex as servicing her husband. This dysfunction is exacerbated if the husband has been or is involved in pornography because he consequently objectifies his wife. His distortion of her fosters her servicing of him. When she begins to deal with the effects of her abuse, she might pull away from any sexual relation in an effort to no longer be controlled. Meanwhile, he believes he has lost something.

Carolyn Maltas and Joseph Shay conducted a study involving childhood sexual abuse victims and their partners, the large majority of whom were married and had children. The abuse survivors in their study did not have vivid memories of their abuse when they became involved with their partner nor did they think that what they did remember was of any consequence. However, recall of the sexual trauma from childhood was often activated by a life event such as marriage and sexual intimacy.[11]

When the couples studied by Maltas and Shay engaged in sexual intimacy, the survivor's recall of the sexual trauma occurred. Furthermore, partners were sometimes "drawn into repeating or reenacting aspects of the abusive relationship."[12] Again, this was often an unconscious process. The focus of the study was the impact of the survivor's childhood sexual trauma on the partner, or husband. Their finding was that the trauma of the survivor was contagious to the partner. Maltas and Shay coined the term *trauma contagion* which refers to "The process by which the trauma is communicated, like a virus, to an intimate sexual partner is thus experienced more pervasively than it is by someone in a close but different kind of relationship to the survivor."[13]

The survivor's "reenactment" of the abuse with the marriage partner sounds absurd and abhorrent to most, and perhaps you as the reader. However, as Patrick Carnes points out, "In part, trauma repetition is an effort by the victim to bring resolution to the trauma. By repeating the experience, the victim tries to figure out a way to respond so the fear can be eliminated."[14] Sadly, however, as Carnes goes on to point out, the traumatic wound is only deepened in the survivor.

As noted earlier, the assumption of many couples entering marriage is that the early childhood experience of the past sexual abuse would have inconsequential impact on the marriage in the present. To the contrary, not only is the past trauma not inconsequential, it is contagious. The assumptions going into the relationship are shattered. As a result, a husband wonders what happened to the woman he married. Will he get his wife back? In some cases, a husband might wonder if he will get his own life back.

## 2. Understand The Ambiguous Nature Of Your Loss

Pauline Boss identifies two kinds of loss in her book, *Ambiguous Loss: Learning to Live with Unresolved Grief.* The first, physical loss and psychological presence, refers to the kind of loss that is easily recognized, such as the death of a loved one. Even though the loved one is physically gone, the presence of the loved one lives on forever (psychologically) in the mind of the grieving person.

The second form of loss, *physical presence and psychological loss* is ambiguous. The loved one of an Alzheimer's patient has the ongoing physical presence of the patient but experiences the psychological loss. The partner may be sitting right in front of you but there is no longer a cognitive connection through such means as a meaningful conversation about world affairs and trends. No longer is there the depth of emotional connection through the intimacy of sharing and understanding deep needs.[15]

Husbands of childhood sexual abuse survivors experience ambiguous loss. As we've noted, the emotional connection is lost or diminished because the survivor's energy is redirected once she begins to process the trauma of the abuse. For example, she is standing next to you, but:

• She feels a million miles away.
• She won't touch you.
• She is not talking to you.
• That's all she does; she just stands there.

This sense of loss is disturbing, and it can feel like rejection. But the first step towards a healthier response to the loss is to understand its ambiguous nature.

### ESTABLISHING NEW PATTERNS

We tend to idealize the past because we somehow forget the difficulties and failures of the past. This may be truer for husbands than for wives. But what we viewed as a good or more preferable marriage in Act I had dysfunctions that we did not recognize at the time.

Now is the time to establish some new patterns of dealing with our loss. The first step is to view this as an opportunity for growth.

### 1. Assess The Past Liabilities And The Present Opportunity

If your wife pursued achievement as a coping mechanism, she was chasing after a mirage in her emotional desert. That was not a healthy way for her to live. As a response to your current situation, consider how you can offer her safety to be who she is today. Grow together in discovering the value of finding our worth in personhood rather than in performance.

In many marriages involving a survivor of childhood sexual abuse, there is the loss of sexual intimacy. At this point, many husbands want to argue, "But sexual intimacy is part of God's plan. Why should I be okay with this loss when God did not intend the loss?" Roger, the husband of a survivor whose relationship was robbed of sexual intimacy echoed the grievance of many husbands when he said, "I've felt cheated!"

True, the loss of sexual intimacy is not what ought to be in God's eyes. But neither is the loss caused by an auto accident that leaves the survivor crippled and unable to physically function in sexual intimacy.

**What we viewed as a good or more preferable**
**marriage in Act I had dysfunctions**
**that we did not recognize at the time.**

Granted, the desire is for growth and that your wife, through wise counsel, can work through the violation of her sexual privacy in the past that vandalizes her sexual intimacy in the present. But this is also a time for growth in you as well. Concentration can be given to deepening emotional and relational intimacy. This may likely mean the growth of ourselves as we seek to fully know and be fully known.

### 2. Accept Your Loss As A Pathway To Growth

Observation of human behavior informs us that there is more than one way to grieve loss; some people progress through their grief and others collapse in their grief. How are you grieving your sense of loss?

In their book, *The Grief Recovery Handbook*, John James and Russell Friedman spoke from their own experience as they outlined the pathway that most of us are conditioned to take when we experience loss.

John was five years old when his dog died. It was heartbreaking because he had done life with the dog. After several days of crying over the loss, John's dad came up with what he thought was the elegant solution. He went into John's room and said, "Don't cry—on Saturday We'll get you a new dog."

Not knowing it, John's dad had taught him the first two principles of how he thought John should handle loss.

Don't cry—*Bury your feelings*
We'll get a new dog—*Replace your losses*

John's second experience of loss came at age fourteen when he was dumped by his girlfriend. One night, John's mom reinforced his two life principles about loss when she said, "Don't feel bad—there are plenty of fish in the sea."

Don't feel bad—*Bury your feelings*
There are plenty of fish in the sea—*Replace your losses*

Years later, John's grandfather died. John saw his mother sobbing in the living room. He wanted to cry with her. But his dad said, "Don't disturb your mother. She'll be okay in a little while." The third and fourth principles of processing loss had now been implanted.

Don't disturb your mother—*Grieve alone*
She'll be okay in a little while—*Time will heal*

As their experiences of loss mounted and the corresponding ill-advised counsel was offered, the authors' conclusion was that **pain could be avoided by not getting close.**

Let's review:

Principle #1: Bury your feelings
Principle #2: Replace your losses
Principle #3: Grieve alone
Principle #4: Let time heal
Principle #5: Avoid pain by not getting too close to others[16]

Our society offers countless ways to bury our pain. Some people engage in addictions and dependencies to stuff down the pain in our lives; drugs and alcohol, work, busyness, shopping, TV, over-eating, etc. All of these are attempts to bury the pain of loss. In marriage, some people use divorce to replace the loss of what they thought they had.

In chapter one, I addressed the dangers of burying our feelings when loss occurs in our marriage relationship. For some, divorce is chosen in an attempt to replace real or perceived loss (e.g., loss of a child, loss of our youth, loss of connection). People believe that once you have a new spouse, you won't have to think about your former spouse anymore. Or, after too great of a loss, some choose to remain married but to disconnect emotionally, and even physically, in order to avoid any further pain.

The common pathway outlined above leads to neither hope nor healing. It is resignation that can result in sadness, sickness, and spoiled relationships. Is there a better pathway?

I have found guidance from reading the Bible. Perhaps it has been different for you. I know that some really struggle with God and therefore have not found any help from reading the scriptures. Perhaps you find God difficult to understand. That's okay. So do I.

Hear me out for a moment. If you and I were able to fully understand God and his ways, then he would be more like us. That would not be a good thing. I don't need a God like me. Secondly, though there are things recorded in the scripture that puzzle me and make me wonder why God allowed it, at least he is totally honest with us. God doesn't hide himself from us. He lays it all out. I need a God who is just like that.

In view of the perspective I've shared, note the pathway laid out in the Psalms. In general, the Psalms follow a basic outline: orientation, disorientation, and reorientation. I suggest these three steps as our pathway in loss. Here's a description of the pathway and verses that depict each phase.

**Step1. Orientation:** the times when you feel like you and God are on the same page and you have found your place in the world; you're adjusted, happy, and filled with gratitude. "The Lord is my shepherd, I lack nothing (Psalm 23:1 NIV)."

**Step 2. Disorientation:** the bottom falls out and you feel sad, robbed, lost and hurt; you wonder, Where is God and what is he doing? This is where the commonly accepted stages of grief—denial, anger, bargaining, depression—occur.[17] "My God, I cry out by day, but you do not answer, by night, but I find no rest (Psalm 22:2 NIV)."

John Townsend, in *Hiding from Love*, stated "Make sadness your ally instead of your enemy… This sadness, or grief, allows you to let go of what you cannot have in order to make room in your heart for what you can have." When a person holds on to lost hopes they become vulnerable to depression. Depression resists processing the loss, whereas lament "moves toward resolving the loss."[18] Solomon spoke of the value of lament: "The mind of the wise is in the house of mourning, while the mind of fools is in the house of pleasure (Ecclesiastes 7:4)."

**Step 3. Reorientation:** you've been through the disorientation, the loss, the hurt, and now you've come through on the other side because you've learned or experienced something about who God really is; you're reoriented. "Taste and see that the LORD is good; blessed is the man who takes refuge in him (Psalms 34:8 NIV)."

The following steps can bring us to a place of reorientation:

a. Acknowledge, mourn, and accept that trauma and loss–including ambiguous loss–are part of this world.
b. Empathize with the loss that your wife has experienced (e.g. her loss of innocence as a child).
c. Let go of the contaminating expectation for a perfect world.
d. Surrender to God's sovereignty as He places us in His larger redemptive story.

The Psalms invite us to embrace and express our grief to God because one thing is absolutely certain—we will get disoriented in this world. Asaph, a guy who lived long ago and experienced severe disorientation said,

> Yes, my spirit was bitter,
> and my insides felt sharp pain.
> I was ignorant and lacked insight;
> I was as senseless as an animal before you.
> But I am continually with you;
> you hold my right hand.
> You guide me by your wise advice,
> and then you will lead me to a position of honor.
> Whom do I have in heaven but you?
> I desire no one but you on earth.
> My flesh and my heart may grow weak,
> but God always protects my heart and gives me stability.
> (Psalm 73:21–26 NET)

People who embrace their loss and express it freely to God, begin the journey that leads them to the realization of freedom and hopefulness. Our natural tendency is to hold on. That's one reason why we become so disoriented, we're trying to hold on to what does not exist, at least in the moment. Only as we grieve and let go of what was can we open space in our lives to be reoriented to what is now.

### 3. Think Again About The Earlier Years Of Your Marriage

The reality is that to "get one's wife back" would be to bring her back to a previous dysfunctional and traumatic existence. What is needed is for the survivor to get help so that maturing and healing can occur. When help is received, the emotional development that was stalled in the trauma can begin to progress toward health. Previous dysfunctional patterns can be uncovered, understood, and overcome. The antidote is for the husband to progress in self–discovery and emotional health as well.

There came a point in our healing process when my wife and I realized that we did not want to go back to Act I of our marriage. Our initial attraction to each other that brought us into marriage certainly included healthy elements. We shared spiritual values. Both of us loved to laugh. I needed her unconventional tendency and she needed my conventional stability. I certainly found her attractive and she thought the same of me. However, the dysfunctional baggage deeply embedded in each of our lives also served as a means of magnetizing us to each other. My controlling nature—a feature whose roots went back to my childhood upbringing—was a dysfunctional match for my wife whose abuse had sadly conditioned her to silently endure the control of another. Our dating and early phase of our Act 1 kept us within the familiar: I exerted dominance and mistook her silent endurance as willing acceptance.

> **There came a point in our healing process**
> **when my wife and I realized that we did not want**
> **to go back to Act I of our marriage.**

Fortunately, growth occurred through counseling and our willingness to adopt new perspectives and practices. We came to the point of not wanting to return to Act 1. We had taken on a new perspective and were employing new patterns.

## CONCLUSION

I'm not sure where the concept originated, but my counselor, Dr. Daniel Green, spoke to me once of the fact that the experiences and growth stages of our lives are like the rings in a tree. A single ring represents our experience today or this year. There are many other rings through which we have grown and there are more to come.

There are certain rings in my past that I wish were not there. They are rings that I don't want to list, and no one would want to love. Though I recall those rings regrettably, God responds to those rings redemptively. I like the words of Brennan Manning,

> It takes a profound conversion to accept that God is relentlessly tender and compassionate toward us just as we are—not in spite of our sins and faults (that would not be total acceptance), but with them. Though God does not condone or sanction evil, He does not withhold His love because there is evil in us.[19]

In other words, it is profound to accept that God takes me as His own—not in spite of various rings in my life (for that would be acceptance with reluctance), but with those unlovable rings in my life. Though He does not condone that ring, He has a way of including that ring in His full redemptive work.

The unlovable rings exist, in our wives as well as in us as husbands. Just as the tree needs each and every element to be what it is and to keep growing, we need each and every aspect of our lives in order to be who God is fashioning us to be. If we reject any of our *rings*, we reject a part of who we are today and what God is shaping for tomorrow. To love me today is to accept all the rings that make me who I am today.

**To love your wife is to: Accept all the rings that make her who she is today. Let go of the one you thought you had.**

## Chapter Two: Personal Application

1. List your losses in your relationship with your wife.

2. List your wife's losses that, to your knowledge, are due to her childhood sexual abuse.

3. How has your grief over your loss followed the common pattern of our society?

4. Whether the loss is permanent or temporary, reorientation puts us on a pathway of releasing and receiving. Thoughtfully work through the following suggested steps. Don't rush through this.

> a. Acknowledge, mourn, and accept that trauma and loss–including ambiguous loss–are part of this world.

> b. Empathize with the loss that your wife has experienced (e.g. her loss of innocence as a child).

> c. Let go of the contaminating expectation for a perfect world.

> d. Surrender to God's sovereignty as He places us in His larger redemptive story.

For a more in-depth review of this chapter, we have also provided a full, free downloadable "Guide for Application" on our website:
www.marriagereconstructionministries.org.
It is our hope that the additional questions in this guide will take you further into potential personal and marital growth.

Chapter Three

# SHOULD I STAY OR SHOULD I GO?

Think back to your wedding day. Like most grooms, you had bright hopes. Hopes for companionship, fun vacations, shared responsibilities in the home, perhaps anticipation for a dream home together, and hopes for intimacy… and, if you were like most grooms, lots of it.

But some of those hopes have likely been shattered if you are reading this chapter. As the husband of a childhood sexual abuse survivor, some of your dreams might have turned into nightmares. Your anticipation of hope has been replaced with a cry for help. Rather than sharing a bed, you might be sleeping on a couch. Instead of building shared memories, you've been battling shared trauma.

When I officiated wedding ceremonies during my forty years of pastoral ministry, my opening remarks to the couple typically included something like this: "Before you lies a future with its hopes and disappointments, pleasures and pain, successes and failures, and its joys and sorrows." If the pastor officiating my wedding said something of that sort, I either entirely missed it or foolishly dismissed it. I thought that marriage was going to open doors of tremendous opportunity and fulfillment. I expected that marriage to my wife was going to make me feel complete for the rest of my life. In my naiveté I was not prepared for reality.

Marriage counselors and researchers offer ample evidence that the long–term effects of childhood sexual abuse have a trajectory that also affects the marriage relationship. The adjustments and conflicts common to marriage become intensified by the abuse. The long–term effects of the abuse impose disappointment, pain, sorrow, and often a sense of failure on both the survivor and her husband. A husband's disappointment and pain can be provoked by numerous factors, including…

- The sense of rejection stemming from his wife's emotional distancing
- Frustration resulting from contradictory behaviors
- Emasculation resulting from a dysfunctional sexual relationship
- Traumatization in dealing with his wife's addictions, eating disorders, or other self–injurious behavior

Husbands who are besieged by the rejection, frustration, emasculation, and traumatization are confronted by a question that they never anticipated on their wedding day: *Should I stay or should I go?*

Husbands who decide to stay can do so from a variety of motivations including theological beliefs, traditional values, and even selfish ambition. Quincy and Wes are both husbands of survivors who had decided to stay when I spoke to them. Quincy spoke of marriage as though it seemingly offered no form of escape when he said, "It's for better or for worse and in good health and poor health. I mean, you're pretty much in it." While Quincy spoke in terms of obligation, Wes spoke in terms that included affection when he said, "I'm committed to my wife. I made promises to her. I said before man and God that I was going to be committed to her. I love her more now than I did when I married her."

Chad's response and attitude to the question of "Should I stay or should I go?" was not so much obligation or affection as it was reputation. His reputation seemed to be on the line when he stated, "It would have been easier to walk. But I didn't want to walk away—that was my wife. I wanted this to be a success in my life. I didn't want to be a failure."

Dan did not see how he could stay without some form of help. He recalled battling the question "Should I stay or should I go?" His motivation for staying was captured in these words:

> *I remember the first time I was just praying about it and really feeling like this is the girl I'm supposed to marry. That saved my marriage and still does now. I feel that… God is saying, "That is the girl you marry." Left to my own devices, I would definitely have divorced by now.*

Just as there are variations in husbands' motivations for staying, there are also variations in the mode of leaving for husbands who choose to go. Nelson's desired mode of leaving was separation. He said, "Divorce doesn't seem like an option, but I've contemplated maybe separating." He had come to believe that his wife, Jan, would be better without him.

Roger's desired mode of leaving was divorce. His view that divorce was a justified option was clear when I asked if he'd ever contemplated divorce and he answered, "Oh, for heaven's sake, yes!" Referring to his marriage, he continued by saying, "I just don't deserve this." Roger was still in the marriage only because divorce was not an option for his wife.

Kurt wished for a more extreme mode of leaving. Though he did not want to opt for divorce, he did reveal his vulnerable prayer.

> *I asked God to take my life. I didn't want to take it myself. I never thought about taking pills and overdosing. I still felt the responsibility for my family. At the same time, I would have relished a heart attack that takes me out in the night. Or, even cancer. I wanted to go out with honor, not with shame. "God, take me in a car wreck, please."*

## EXPLORING A NEW PERSPECTIVE

No reliable statistics are available of the percentage of divorces attributable to childhood sexual abuse. However, ample resources give evidence of the tensions and strife that can exist in a marital relationship involving a survivor of childhood sexual abuse. In addition to the individual effects of trauma upon the survivor, there are also the interpersonal problems that include sexual dysfunction, communication problems, and challenges to emotional intimacy.

There is research that indicates a repeated association between a history of childhood sexual abuse and lower relationship stability and longevity that eventually terminates in separation or divorce. Women with a history of sexual abuse had a higher rate of "transitory unions," unions that were typically short cohabitations with only brief periods of time in each union.[20]

## Research indicates a repeated association between a history of childhood sexual abuse and lower relationship stability and longevity

Courtright and Rogers, husbands of childhood sexual abuse survivors, told their stories and outlined four options for how husbands might cope with the struggles of his wife's trauma:

- Option One: Choosing to quit (i.e., divorce)
- Option Two: Choosing to win, in which the assertiveness of the husband mirrored the original sexual abuse when the perpetrator forced his will.
- Option Three: Choosing to lose, in which the husband concedes rather than secedes (as in choosing to quit).
- Option Four: Choosing to adapt. By adapting to "our unfamiliar and often frightening situations, we began forging relationships with our wives that exceeded our expectations." Though the adapting was difficult, prolonged, and spotted with headache and heartache, the process resulted in "stronger, deeper, more satisfying relationships with our wives.[21]

Dan learned of his wife's abuse three months into their dating relationship. His impression was, "It was a data point. I was ignorant of what [childhood sexual abuse] meant and what it was going to mean for us. It just was like, 'ok, great.' It was input…"

But the data became trauma after they got to their hotel room on their wedding night. Up to that point, both Dan and his wife Nikki had great expectations for intimacy. They had saved themselves physically in their relationship for this moment. But the anticipated pleasure became unexpected pain. Nikki broke down into tears when Dan began to unzip her dress. Dan recalled the moment by saying,

> I remember thinking, "How did I end up here? I'm in my tux on my wedding night, and this is not a good sign. This is not what I thought it was going to be."

The disappointment, pain, and sorrow that Dan and other husbands experience can mount up to a burdensome load and a troublesome marriage.

Dan's early realization that his marriage was not going to be what he anticipated led him to the reality of the four options proposed by Courtright and Rogers. He could quit, fight to win, concede to losing, or adapt. He opted to adapt by choosing to consider his marriage as the arena for personal growth and transformation. He captured his personal and marital turning point in this statement:

> *I know now that God obviously didn't want the abuse to happen. But He's used that in my life. The primary means for sanctification [i.e., personal and spiritual growth] in my life is my marriage. I think, given my background and my tendencies, sexuality would be first and foremost, like sexual intimacy with my wife would be on the top of the list and everything else would take a second seat to it. And how I'm looking at it now is like, you know what, God knew that. He gave Nikki to me in a way that she's to make me more Christ-like. And of all things, even now, I'm like, "Why that? Why that?" But, in those times, I can be like, "All right, you know what? God, your plan is perfect." And this side of the grave, I'm not going to get it. I may buck against it, but ultimately that's what He is doing.*
>
> *I'm confident knowing the primary means of sanctification in my life is my marriage. And it's not to rob me; it's not to deny me. And it's changed dramatically from what it was.*

Dan and Nikki both worked at their marriage. Dan made himself accountable to guys who had his best interest in mind and were not afraid to speak boldly into his life. Nikki became involved in a support group for childhood sexual abuse survivors through their church. Dan and Nikki adapted together because of the individual transformation that was occurring in each of them. A changed marriage for Dan and Nikki meant that neither could continue in the marriage as they had been.

My personal stance is to do everything possible to preserve and nurture the marriage union. I believe that the union of one man and one woman is the design of God. This is not to say that all are to marry but that those who do marry enter into a union that is sacred, meaning that it is intended by God to be different from any other union. As such, severing any marital union results in wounds to the individuals who were bonded together by that sacred union.

Therefore, I caution husbands to guard against following the siren call and illusive notion of the culture "to be true to themselves." Have you ever given thought to what the phrase "be true to yourself" means?

I personally believe we must consider the possibility that this notion of being true to ourselves might be an illusion that covers my hidden expectation to have circumstances always go my way. This expectation might be put in terms of "I deserve more" or "Life should be easier and more fun." *This expectation will make me a consumer rather than a lover.*

Which of us does not want life to be easier and more fun? Yet would we ever be able to convince anyone that expectations for ease and fun are marks of maturity? As one husband of a survivor put it, "I'm challenged by my inner struggle of selfishness and desire while knowing that God has called me to love her unconditionally and to be her protector and ally." *This conviction will make me a lover rather than a consumer.*

Sadly, the insidious violation and invasion of childhood sexual abuse can inflict deep wounds upon the survivor that result in distorted perceptions of God, self, man, sexuality, and life. When the distortions are not countered with truth and love, survivors are often left to spin into a downward spiral of darkness, despair, and destructive choices. While the response of some survivors is aversion to sexual activity, the response of others can be perversion through sexual promiscuity. Perhaps your wife has chosen another man or woman, or maybe even other men or women. In such cases, it can be deduced that she has chosen to go. Your role may be to let go. This may not be your *preferred* option, but it may be the *imposed* option.

Situations for when divorce or separation might be unavoidable and warranted include the following:

- When your health or safety, or that of your children, is at risk due to the lifestyle choices of your wife.
- When a period of separation can give "breathing room" to address individual issues of dysfunction or immaturity before entering counseling as a couple to resolve relational issues.

- When your wife has chosen to leave in order to live with
  another person.
- When your wife has chosen to leave and completely shuts the door
  on any possibility of reconciliation.

## ESTABLISHING NEW PATTERNS

Marriage is a union of a man and a woman. Marital unity engages the cooperation of both husband and wife. Sadly, some survivors of childhood sexual abuse resist long–term union as well as any counseling to ensure that union.

Dr. Daniel Green maintains that we are responsible for two things and not responsible for three others:

- We are responsible for how we treat others.
- We are responsible for how we treat ourselves.
- We are not responsible for how others treat others.
- We are not responsible for how others treat us.
- We are not responsible for how others treat themselves.

The effects of childhood sexual abuse imprinted relational withdrawal and sexual promiscuity on Jan. She emotionally ran from her church, her children, and her husband and sexually ran to other men. She had multiple affairs and abortions. Nelson, her husband, gave his best effort in remaining steadfast in his marriage. The question to be answered was whether he could remain in a marriage that Jan had continuously refused by her actions. Though he was responsible to love and honor Jan, he could not be responsible for her breach of their marriage bond.

*Should I stay or should I go?* In some cases, wives who are survivors of childhood sexual abuse are the ones who answer the question by choosing to go.

Whatever a husband's—or wife's—answer might be to the question, there are some perceptions and patterns to be considered before making any decision.

## 1. Do You See Your Wife As The Only One Having The Problem?

Families of childhood sexual abuse survivors are often prone to adopt a selective perception. With our selective perception, we interpret information and situations in ways that are congruent with our existing beliefs. For example, people who vote for a political candidate who ends up being elected to office will often view the elected politician's actions favorably so as to be congruent with their pre–election beliefs and expectations. Likewise, those who voted for the defeated candidate will view the elected politician with disfavor. The selective perception serves as evidence to them that they voted correctly. In other words, we see things the way we want to see them so that we can prove ourselves to be correct in our views. Husbands whose wives are survivors of childhood sexual abuse are often culpable of selective perceptions.

> **. . . we see things the way we want to see them so that we can prove ourselves to be correct in our views.**

An example of selective perception is when the husband of a survivor views his wife as the "identified patient." An identified patient is the one who is identified by others as the individual having the problem.

Many of the detrimental and dysfunctional effects imposed upon a wife who is the survivor of childhood sexual abuse can "convince" her husband that she has the problem and is therefore identified as the patient—the one in need of some therapeutic care. His selective perception that his wife is the identified patient can also serve as convincing evidence to him that he and his wife have "grown apart" or that they were not meant for each other in the first place, and that he should therefore pursue divorce.

> **Many of the detrimental and dysfunctional effects imposed upon a wife who is the survivor of childhood sexual abuse can "convince" her husband that she has the problem and is therefore identified as the patient—the one in need of some therapeutic care.**

The effects of childhood sexual abuse include eating disorders, panic attacks, substance abuse, self–injurious behavior, and anxiety disorder. These effects do, in fact, necessitate therapeutic care. But husbands who do not struggle with these particular effects exercise selective perception when they scan their wives' daily behavior for proof that she has a problem. And though he has issues of his own, he is unable to identify how his issues too cause mounting harm to the marriage. In his selective perception, he has a running monologue of "If only" thoughts in his mind: "If only she would go to a counselor," "If only she would just decide to move on," "If only she could not get so angry," "If only I could afford a lawyer to get a divorce."

### 2. If Your Wife Is The Identified Patient, Is She The Only Patient?

Fred approaches his wife, Linda, at the end of the day and embraces her. In response, she stiffens—not because of Fred but because of her current shame and self-rejection. Linda feels unlovable. In response to her stiffness, Fred feels pushed away. So he backs away, sullenly goes into another room, and turns on the TV. For the rest of the evening, he counters Linda's stiffness with a dose of his own stiffness by never looking directly at her. With selective perception, he sulks, thinking that she is a cold—and sometimes even cruel—person, that he would be less lonely being divorced and alone. Is there only one patient in this case?

Jack struggles with Lisa's aversion to sexual intimacy and therefore rationalizes indulging himself in some pornography. In reality, he indulged in pornography long before his struggle with Lisa, but her aversion to sexual intimacy now serves his selective perception. He persuades himself that he has cause for his current behavior due to her cold behavior. He envisions the women who seem to be so eager to engage in sexual adventure and never seem to push a man away. He thinks, "There must be some woman out there who would admire and appreciate me. So should I stay or should I go?"

In a counseling session, Jack learns that his involvement in pornography has rewired his thinking and behavior so that he objectifies women. When he engages sexually with Lisa, she senses the objectification, which repels her because it repeats the objectification of her perpetrator when she was sexually abused as a child. In the counseling session, is there only one "identified" patient?

Twenty-three-year-old Jackie struggled with a sense of powerlessness due to the sexual abuse from her older brother when she was a young teen. He was strong and aggressive. She was petite and powerless. At the fitness center, she notices Derrick, who is strong and attractive. Derrick moves from one fitness apparatus to another with precision and determination. His body language speaks control. He pays attention to Jackie, and she becomes drawn to his strength and his control of life. He functions at work with the same precision that he performs in fitness. They marry. But a year into their marriage, Derrick's selective perception focuses on Jackie's powerlessness and he becomes exasperated with her passiveness. He exerts himself as though enticing her to fight back.

However, she wilts under Derrick's oppressive power and dominance. He stands over Jackie in such a way that she cannot move. His relentless insistence that things operate his way at home mirrors his relentless persistence in his workout. He privately wonders how he got involved with such a weak woman and if he made a huge mistake in marrying her.

The traits that drew Jackie to Derrick now repel her. What is the identified problem in this case: her powerlessness or his dominance? Who is the patient that has brought the problem to this relationship?

When a husband's selective perception labels his wife as the identified patient, he diminishes her sense of self-worth. But that is not all. His selective perception actually functions as self-deception. By seeing his wife as having the problems, he can distract himself from any of his own problematic attitudes and behaviors.

## His selective perception actually functions as self-deception.

### 3. Is My Decision To Divorce Being Driven By The Deception Of Selective Perception?

One way to avoid the deception is to do some introspection. Before making any decision about staying or going, husbands of survivors make healthier choices when they first choose self-examination rather than selectively perceiving their wife as the sole patient. If a husband fails to look inward, he will be at risk for making decisions that will not only lead to different relationships but also repeated patterns.

I don't know the origin of this question, but it is a question that should be asked by everyone: *"What is it like to be on the other side of me?"*

**If a husband fails to look inward, he will be at risk
for making decisions that will not only lead to different
relationships but also repeated patterns.**

Right now, step into the arena of your conflict and ask that question. Go back to the most recent conflict with your wife and ask the question. Look through her eyes. Go back to your most recent conflict at work. How did you seem to others?

These inquiries won't guarantee a truthful answer. Selective perception will fight the truth about ourselves. Our vision will be filled with "Yes, buts." "Yes, but she doesn't talk." "Yes, but she doesn't seem to care." "Yes, but the people at work are incompetent." Whether those accusations are true or not, see them as your perceptions.

In your search for truth, be aware that your selective perception may lead you to others with the same selective perception. Generally, family members won't give us an accurate portrayal of ourselves when assessing whether the issues lie within our spouse or us. Siblings will generally have selective perceptions that favor their own family unit over in-laws.

It is most beneficial when we have two or three friends who have our best interest in mind and can lovingly speak to us with wisdom, grace, and truth. If you do not have this kind of friend, then it's time to ask yourself why that is the case. "Faithful are the wounds of a friend (Proverbs 27:6)."

I've been guilty of selective perception in a big way. I saw the effects of abuse in my wife and was convinced that she needed her counselor's help. She did not argue with that. However, just as a family's functioning might revolve around the care of a quadriplegic, I considered that my life was to revolve around my wife and her care. When I told her that I lived for her happiness—I did not verbalize that it was because she was the identified patient—I was bamboozled when she informed me that I was smothering her.

My counselor brought me to the understanding that I had so lost my identity in my wife that I lost all self-awareness of what was true about my own wishes, desires, and perceptions. I was therefore unable to offer intimacy to her.

Intimacy is knowing and being known. I was not able to be known because I did not know myself. I was robbing her of me.

My dysfunctional patterns—which I had not seen due to selective perception and viewing my wife as the identified patient—began and continue to be dismantled and replaced with healthier perspectives and patterns. It can happen.

Men who divorce, ignoring their own issues and dysfunctions, end up running right back into the same cyclical patterns. Better to engage in introspection than to descend into insanity, "doing the same thing over and over again and expecting different results.[22]

### 4. Is My Decision Based On Healthy Expectations?

Tension, trauma, and despair can intrude a marriage affected by childhood sexual abuse. Before pursuing some form of termination to your marriage, you will benefit by considering the terms of marriage.

- What am I expecting from my marriage relationship?
- What am I expecting from my wife?
- What is the basis of my expectations?
- Are my expectations based on some core values or on some cultural whims?

Let's consolidate all those questions into one:

*Am I expecting my marriage to make me happy?*

Has my wife brought me some happiness? For sure! Have I enjoyed happy times in our marriage? Absolutely! But any expectation I have that I will be sustained through the happiness experienced from my wife or my marriage will soon lead me into deep disappointment. The nature of happiness does not allow me to find it on a continual basis from anyone or anything.

Happiness comes from the fifteenth–century Middle English word *hap*, which means "chance." In other words, happiness depends on what, by chance, happens. By its very nature, happiness can be elusive and unpredictable. It cannot be certain. It is subject to what happens, by chance, in my health, friendships, possessions, achievements, and on and on. It is spontaneous because it is all by chance.

To expect that my wife, or my marriage, or anything else will make me happy will eventually, and even persistently, lead me to disappointment.

Chance does not allow for them to have a perfect batting average. Strikeouts will occur. Sickness comes. Moods change, just like mine. Misunderstandings occur. Interruptions invade and minds change.

Rather than pursue happiness, which is dependent upon outward situations, I am wiser to consider my inner decisions. I've been reading David Brooks' *The Road to Character*, in which he reminds us of Viktor Frankl, a Jewish psychiatrist who was sent by the Nazis to the concentration camps. Frankl had lost his wife, mother, and brother to the cruelties of the camps, and he himself was subjected to its tortuous work and beatings. Brooks observes that it became clear to Frankl "that what sort of person he would wind up being depended upon what sort of inner decision he would make in response to his circumstances."[23]

Brooks challenges us with the question of what inner decisions we are making in response to our circumstances and what sort of person we will be[come] as a result of those decisions.

### CONCLUSION

When we judge someone—when we judge someone as the identified patient—we are not seeing who he or she is; instead, we are seeing their effect upon us.

Selective perception can misguide a husband's thinking and even find its expression in such statements to his wife as "Here we go again." I think I've done that a time or two. In other words, we are thinking, "Here we go again… this is just like what you've done or thought before. It doesn't change." Whether or not that is true, it seems to be true most of the time that the biggest frustration for us as husbands is in how we are being affected.

Granted, there are frustrations for husbands. But there are also frustrations for our wives. We are affected, but so are they. In our frustration, it can be enlightening to step away from the tension for a moment and ask ourselves these questions:

- How am I being affected, and how much is that the issue for me?
- How is all this affecting her? What is it like for her?
- Am I avoiding a problem or a need to change because I only see how this affects me?

• Though this affects me, is this really about me? If so, how do I need to change? If this is not about me, how can I respond with calm so that I do not escalate the situation?

If you've discerned that divorce or separation is unavoidable or warranted, I enter with you into the heartache. This is not what either you or your wife ever thought would happen when you stood before the pastor or judge to be united in marriage. My prayer for you is that personal healing and hope will come and that your wife will in some way experience the same.

In the same way that I advise couples not to rush into marriage, I offer to you the caution to not rush into a divorce. Assuming that you've allowed a pastor and/or counselor to speak into your life, I hope you've carefully considered the questions in this chapter so that you can be protected from the possibility of your current decision not only leading you to a different relationship, but also a repeated pattern.

If you've decided to stay, I hope that you have carefully considered the questions in this chapter so that you can be protected from current unhealthy patterns in your marriage being due to unresolved personal issues. My prayer for you is the same as for those who have chosen to terminate their relationship: that personal healing and hope will come and that your wife will in some way experience the same. God, before whom you made your vow, is the only One who can transform and empower us for healthy living, personally and relationally.

Yes, there are seemingly unreasonable, unfavorable, and unpredictable events that occur in marriages that have been inflicted with the effects of childhood sexual abuse. The question is whether we will seek to become someone we never thought possible.

**What inner decisions are we making in response to our circumstances, and what sort of person will we become as a result of these decisions?**

# Chapter Three: Personal Application

1. Up to this point in your relationship, what has been your motive for staying with your wife?

2. What thoughts have you entertained about leaving?

3. Take some time to process and answer these additional questions that were presented in the conclusion of this chapter.

    a. How am I being affected, and how much is that the issue for me?

    b. How is all this affecting her? What is it like for her?

    c. Am I avoiding a problem or a need to change because I only see how this affects me?

    d. Though this affects me, is this really about me? If so, how do I need to change? If this is not about me, how can I respond with calm so that I do not escalate the situation?

For a more in-depth review of this chapter, we have also provided a full, free downloadable "Guide for Application" on our website: www.marriagereconstructionministries.org.
It is our hope that the additional questions in this guide will take you further into potential personal and marital growth.

Chapter Four:

# WHY DOESN'T GOD HEAL MY WIFE?

Whatever their spiritual beliefs may be, most people do pray. So, assuming that you pray, I have a question. Have you wondered why God sometimes seems silent and slow to respond? I have!

My wife disclosed her childhood sexual abuse to me ten years into our marriage. Everything changed that night, except me. I remained as I was—ignorant and arrogant. I was ignorant of the effects of childhood sexual abuse and, at the time, I was even oblivious to the consequences that those effects were imposing on our marriage.

In addition to my ignorance, I was arrogant—too arrogant to make sure she received the appropriate care. In my mind, mental health professions were for the weak, not us. We had received some initial pastoral counsel that I thought should suffice. I was not aware of my pride, and I would not admit my fears.

My wife's appeals for help fell on my deaf ears. I was too self–centered and self–protective to offer her the support she deserved and the help she desired. Tragically, her emotional and physical health slowly unraveled as she began dealing with the hideous reality of what for years had been stuffed within her consciousness.

After eight years of my resistance, some dear friends of ours urged us to see a psychiatrist that had been very helpful to them. By this time, I was desperate enough to agree and set up the appointment. By the time we saw the psychiatrist, my wife had gone consecutive weeks without sleep.

We sank comfortably into the leather couch in the psychiatrist's office on a Tuesday morning. My wife looked terrific. To the untrained eye, her colorful dress and appearance masqueraded the darkness within. But our doctor saw beyond the beauty to her brokenness. Neither my wife nor I were prepared for the psychiatrist's decision. Within a very brief time of meeting with him, he said, "I'm going to admit you to the psychiatric ward. Bill, I want you to go home and get her the clothes that she needs." That day was the first of an unanticipated four–week hospitalization and relentless journey.

Like most people who are in despair, we began reading the Psalms of David. My wife and I agreed together that we'd read and absorb one chapter for each day. I thought that was a good plan. There are 150 chapters in the Psalms. In my naiveté, I thought that the ordeal should certainly be over in five months.

One thing that is difficult for husbands of survivors to accept is that we are part of the system. To put it more bluntly, just as there are complementary attractions that bring a couple together, there are also complementary dysfunctions that match couples together. This journey was going to require that I too receive counsel in order to do the necessary self–examination and transformation for my own development.

After her four–week stay in the psychiatric ward, she came home. It was awkward. Life would never be the same. I did not yet understand that the familiar patterns of the past could no longer be the accepted patterns for the future.

### ...the familiar patterns of the past could no longer be the accepted patterns for the future.

Five months went by. We were done reading the daily chapters from the Psalms, but we were not anywhere near the finish line. My wife's life revolved around her weekly counseling appointments. They were emotionally exhausting, but they were also what kept her going. Tears and fear engulfed her on the rare occasions that an appointment was cancelled or not scheduled by her psychiatrist; the appointments were her lifeline.

The weekly appointments with my psychologist functioned as stress relievers for me. His office was dimly lit with light classical music softly playing. I sat in the chair next to his desk and spewed out my frustration, much like letting some air out of an overfilled tire that is ready to explode.

Each week, my counselor gently offered an insight or idea that I could instill and implement as part of my life. I thought I was making great strides in becoming a supportive husband.

I began asking God to bring emotional healing to my wife. I thought He would get a lot of glory if He did heal her. Many people were watching our process and tracking our progress. Moreover, it did not make sense that my wife should be the one suffering in her innocence.

## ...it did not make sense that my wife should be the one suffering in her innocence.

I'd get a lot of relief too if God brought healing, though I did not say that or pray that out loud. I was agonizing over the unpredictable behavior, her constant sleeping, listlessness, depression, isolation, nightmares, physical problems, fears, dissociation, and suicidal thoughts.

I prayed for a miracle of instantaneous healing, thinking it would be a Win/Win/Win: God would win the glory, my dear wife would win freedom from all the pain, and I'd win back a *normal* life again. (See Chapter One, *What is a normal marriage anyway?*)

### EXPLORING A NEW PERSPECTIVE

If your wife was sexually abused as a child, I'm guessing you've prayed for the miracle of God's healing as well. Sometimes God does perform a miracle, delivering survivors of childhood sexual abuse from all of its cruel effects. In my work with men, I remember Chad and Barb, who sought psychiatric help but only saw Barb's condition worsen. They pursued the option of what is often referred to as a "deliverance ministry" and testified of complete deliverance for Barb that occurred instantaneously. At the same time, I know of other couples for whom the deliverance theology and methodology led to a worsened condition for the survivor, resulting in the need for psychiatric care and hospitalization.

The variance of how God works rests in His sovereignty. The historical and personal accounts in Scripture exhibit the various ways God performed His work and purpose at His own choosing. Some were instantaneously healed. I think of the man with leprosy who came to Jesus, got down on his knees, and begged, "If you are willing, you can make me clean." God knows—literally—that I had knelt and begged innumerable times, sometimes with a good friend joining me in the petitioning. For the leper, Jesus reached out

His hand, touched the man, and said He was willing to do so. "Immediately the leprosy left him and he was cleansed (Mark 1:42)." I wondered why Jesus would not do the same for my wife.

For others, Jesus interacted with the sick during the process of healing. There was a blind man whom others brought to Jesus (Mark 8:22–25). They did the begging that Jesus would touch the man. Jesus took the blind man by the hand and led him outside the village. If I had been that blind man, I would have felt quite unsettled. Many of us who live with some level of shame would guess that we were going to receive a reprimand once we were out of the public view. Whatever it was that the blind man was anticipating, he never could have expected to be on the receiving end of Jesus' saliva.

Then Jesus asked, "Do you see anything?" Are you kidding? How would you answer? I know how I might have answered. "Ah, just a minute, Jesus. Maybe once I get this spit out of my eye. Do you have any goggles I can wear?"

Mark gives us the answer of what the blind man actually told Jesus. He said, "I see people; they look like trees walking around."

So, Jesus continued the process of healing by covering the man's eyes with his hands. Mark tells us, "Jesus put his hands on the man's eyes. Then his eyes were opened, his sight was restored, and he saw everything clearly (v. 25)."

Husbands of childhood sexual abuse survivors can learn a lot from Jesus' interaction with the blind man. First, God sometimes chooses to do His work with us in solitude. God does not need to do things to get the glory of the crowd, as I had thought. And though we as husbands of survivors often feel very much alone because others are not really able to grasp our situation, we do have Someone who is with us. As Brennan Manning has pointed out, *the resurrected Christ of the past is our incomparable companion of the present.*[24]

Jesus wants time alone with us, and we need the one–on–one time with Him. It is in these times of solitude with Him that He addresses our personal need in an individually selected manner. He will not do for me just as He has done for someone else. That would be like the relative who gives everyone identical handmade gifts at Christmas. There's nothing special or personal about that which is distributed to all in the same way. God wants to make His unique mark in each of us. He refuses to treat any of us just like anyone else.

This brings us to the second truth husbands can learn from Jesus' interaction with the blind man. Don't try to guess how God is going to answer your prayer. Yes, go ahead and make your petition. God gives us freedom to express the desires of our heart, but it's not like He needs our ideas. And in addition to not being able to guess, it is very likely that we are not going to understand how He is going to work. I often need to remind myself of the simply stated truth that someone has made—*God is God and I am not.*

The third truth is that it's going to take longer than I want it to take. This is not because God cannot work faster. His choice of timing is because there is too much for me to learn, and He doesn't want to back up the truck and dump everything on me at once. Notice that Jesus did not inform His disciples about the cross on the day that He called them to follow. The importance of the cross would lead us to believe that Jesus would have communicated that event right away. But the agony of the cross called for merciful timing in how He brought His disciples to understanding—and even then, they were slow to understand.

Fourth, Jesus' incremental work is a perfecting work. Why didn't Jesus just put His hands on the man's eyes in the first place? All I can assume—drawing from my own experience of His work in my life—is that He chooses process in order to perfect.

As I mentioned earlier, I thought I was making great strides in being a supportive husband. But we are most in need when we don't know what we don't know. Therefore, in my own journey, God chose to use a long-term process.

**Four Lessons From Mark 8**

1. *God sometimes does His work in us through solitude.*
2. *Don't try to guess how God will answer your prayer.*
3. *It's going to take longer than you want it to take.*
4. *Jesus' incremental work is His perfecting work.*

If God had instantaneously healed my wife from the wounds and effects of childhood sexual abuse as I wanted Him to do and asked Him to do, neither my wife nor I would have experienced the inner transformation that has brought us to greater freedom. I did not realize that it would be years of periodic counseling before I would begin to understand concepts such as empathy and individuation. It would be more than two decades before I would comprehend the error of seeing my wife as the "identified patient." Am I a slow learner? Probably. But the journey of self–discovery is rarely on a freeway. There are narrow roads, hairpin turns, and detours that must be navigated in the process.

There are no shortcuts. Any hope of my wife and I experiencing a healthy marriage required my personal growth as much as her personal growth.

## ESTABLISHING NEW PATTERNS

We love it when we're standing in line at the grocery store and a new lane opens up so that we don't have to wait. Most of us love express lanes on the freeway and any form of quick check–in at the airport. We want to move from Point A to Point B as quickly as possible.

Likewise, long lines, delayed flights, and slow service at the restaurant test our patience. Waiting for test result from the doctor or waiting for a job interview can be tormenting. Waiting vexes the core of our natural human nature.

Given our nature, God works in our lives and circumstances in ways that test our patience. It seems to be a major theme in His interactions with us. Consider just a few of the biblical examples. Abraham and Sarah waited decades for the child God promised to them. David waited years between the time that God anointed him as king and he actually became king. The Israelites waited centuries for the promised Messiah. In the New Testament, the disciples were to wait and not do anything in Jerusalem until the Holy Spirit was given.

In addition to the living examples are the numerous occasions of instruction to wait. During a time of trouble, God spoke to Israel through David saying, "Wait for the LORD; be strong and take heart and wait for the LORD (Psalm 27:14)." Parents often ask their children, "How many times do I need to remind you?" God, as our heavenly Father, knows the answer to that question in regard to us His children. Often! Here in one verse, God repeats the command. I cannot count the times that I thought I had waited enough. In those moments, God reminds us of the need to continue waiting.

Let's pause here. Before going further, I need to examine our motives more deeply. I am assuming that your faith is in God and that you believe He can bring healing. I am also assuming that your desire is to honor Him with your life. I am assuming that you want His will as well as His work. If that is not the case, then we are simply using God as some magician in the sky.

So, take a moment for personal inventory of your motives because the rest of this chapter assumes your desire to be in union with God rather than at odds with Him.

Scripture makes it clear that waiting before God is prerequisite to experiencing God. The prophet Isaiah teaches that, if we are going to walk with God, we need to learn to wait for Him. Isaiah says, "Since before time began no one has ever imagined, no ear heard, no eye seen, a God like you who works for those who wait for him (Isaiah 64:4)."

Our waiting is not because God is lagging behind. Rather, our waiting is because God is currently at work chiseling away the rougher edges of our life in order to further conform us to His character.

I like how my friend Kirk Livingston articulated this idea by saying, "It's easy to see how waiting has a shaping effect. One cannot help but be shaped during the waiting." Kirk went on to explain that during the waiting there is "The adjustment of expectations [and] the readjustment of desire. Waiting stirs reexamination of nearly everything."[25]

Had God granted an instantaneous healing for my wife, had God not made me wait, I'd be the same ignorant and arrogant husband that I was earlier in our marriage. Probably even worse. That would not suffice, and our marriage would not have survived. The chiseling work and fashioning hand of God removed some of my character flaws and shaped my understanding so that empathy could be developed in my life.

Here are two key and clear distinctions of thought and behavior that God fashioned in me during the waiting.

## 1. Miracle vs. Magic

Kurtz & Ketcham state that "**miracles** involve openness to mystery, the welcoming of surprise, the acceptance of those realities over which we have no control."[26] Jesus' mother, Mary, learned this when Jesus performed His first miracle at the wedding in Cana (John 2). She tried to control Jesus but had to relinquish that control in order for the miracle to occur. **Magic**, on the other hand, is "the attempt to be in control, to manage everything."[27] Mary was not asking for a miracle; she was asking for magic. She wanted to be in control.

When I prayed for God to do a miracle for my wife, I was actually seeking magic. I wanted to return to a sense—as false as it was—that I would once again be in control of life. *Away with the inconvenience of wounds from childhood sexual abuse!* I wanted out from under the cloud of depression. I wanted my wife to be able to function again. I sorely longed for her companionship, of which I had been robbed by her hours of sleep. I wanted my daughters to have again the fun-loving mom they had known in earlier years. Away with hurt and pain!

I did love my wife as best I knew how during the darkest years of her journey. And I was not completely selfish. I wanted her to be free from the pain and trauma she was enduring. But the reality was that my request was also a desire for God to do some magic for me. I wanted order restored so that I could once again live in the illusion that I was in control.

> **I wanted order restored so that I could once again**
> **live in the illusion that I was in control.**

I had to surrender any attempt to be in control, to accept the idea that I am the passenger and not the driver. God is the driver, and I needed to say "Yes" to where He was taking me and the route He was choosing to get there.

My controlling nature had been most evident in our marriage during its initial decades. I did not have to exert very much pressure to be in control. Remember that as a survivor of childhood sexual abuse, my wife had been conditioned to be controlled. So, she did not resist me. I therefore thought that we had a great marriage. I was in charge, and she followed along.

It deeply bothered me the day that her psychiatrist called me a "jack-ass." Though that was the exception of how he spoke to me, I had to come to grips with its measure of truth. I began waking up to the fact that I was living with an incredibly intelligent and talented wife who was to be honored by me. I began discovering that I was not always right and, more importantly, that I did not need to be right.

Was my wife's healing delayed because I had so much to learn? I don't believe so. We were both learning and being transformed by the fashioning hand of God, our divine Sculptor. Our part was to adjust together by establishing the new patterns.

One change in our relationship was more conversation and less control, creating understanding and respect for each other's perspective. My demanding nature dissipated as we learned to sit together in stress–free environments—cafes are our preference—and enjoy conversations together over coffee. This has become one of the most rewarding aspects of our marriage.

None of this mutual growth would have occurred with a miracle. God does work miracles. But He will not perform magic.

### 2. Process vs. Instantaneous

Dr. Archibald Hart wrote about deliverance and therapy. The insights he shared in his article have transformed my life for the past twenty–five years. He acknowledged that the damage done to the psyche through atrocities such as childhood sexual abuse need to be healed. He noted that God sometimes intervenes to erase the scars but that there are many times when supernatural intervention does not occur. His observation as a clinical psychologist was that we are often better off having "worked through" the problems rather than experiencing an instantaneous work from God. Hart contended that our faith increases and deepens more through God's process of healing than through instantaneous healing (p. 75).[28]

> **Our faith increases and deepens more through**
> **God's process of healing than through**
> **instantaneous healing. (A. Hart)**

Dan's wife, Nikki, was a survivor of childhood sexual abuse. He had contended with many of the effects that the abuse imposed on Nikki's life such as distrust and aversion to sexual intimacy.

Dan's experience supported Hart's notion about the value of the process. Speaking of Nikki's abuse and the healing process, Dan said that God "used that in my life. It's the primary means for emotional and spiritual growth in my life and in my marriage."

My response to Dan was "Same for me!"

My relationship with God has been the greatest factor in my development as the husband that my wife desires. When we grow in our faith in God, we discover that life does not revolve around us and we can still be okay.

In the past, I would sulk when things did not go my way. I never yelled at my wife, but I succeeded in penalizing her with my sulking. Unknowingly, it was demeaning to my wife.

On the other hand, my wife knows that she is safest when I am leaning hard into God, yielding my will and trusting Him. Safety is one of the greatest gifts that a husband, whose wife is a survivor of childhood sexual abuse, can give to his wife.

Growing in our faith in God is a lifelong process. Growing in faithfulness knows no shortcuts.

> *But as for me, I watch in hope for the LORD,*
> *I wait for God my Savior;*
> *my God will hear me.*
> *(Micah 7:7)*

# Chapter Four: Personal Application

1. If you read this chapter, I assume God has not chosen to instantaneously heal your wife. If my assumption is accurate, revisit the lessons learned from the healing of the blind man in The Gospel of Mark, chapter 8.

- God sometimes chooses to do His work in with us in solitude (i.e., Jesus wants one–on–one time with us).

- Don't try to guess how God is going to answer your prayer.

- It is going to take longer than we want it to take.

- Jesus' incremental work is a perfecting work.

2. How have these lessons depicted your own experience?

For a more in-depth review of this chapter, we have also provided a full, free downloadable "Guide for Application" on our website: www.marriagereconstructionministries.org.
It is our hope that the additional questions in this guide will take you further into potential personal and marital growth.

Chapter Five:

# WHEN WILL THIS BE OVER?

I've recently been meeting with Daryl, who has been married to Annette for over fifteen years. She had disclosed her childhood sexual abuse two months before our first conversation.

As can be common among survivors of childhood sexual abuse, Annette's effects included aversion to intimacy, especially physical and sexual intimacy. Daryl was prepared to adjust to this void for a season, but he was already wondering how long her distancing herself from him would last.

Many of you are thinking to yourself, "Daryl is not going to like the answer." You know that the struggle and journey can last for not only months but also years.

Husbands married to survivors of childhood sexual abuse want to know where they are on the journey of healing and when they'll get to the destination where all her issues will be resolved. So they ask these questions:

*When will this finally be over?*
*When will we get through this?*
*How long will this take?*

The emotional pain for wives as survivors of childhood sexual abuse and for husbands as *secondary survivors* is often intolerable.[29] So we ask the questions—I sure have—hoping to find out how long this painful journey will last. There don't seem to be any "mile markers," and if there were, it seems that we are still at mile zero. I lost count of the times that my wife's psychiatrist told me to just be patient.

It's natural to ask these questions. After all, who likes pain? But it's also natural for babies to poop in their diapers. Just because it's natural doesn't mean that it's desirable. It occurs to me that my two daughters asked the same questions from the back seat of our car when they were preschoolers: "When will this trip finally be over?" It was natural for them to ask the question, especially on a long trip. As natural as the inquiry into duration may be, we must entertain the notion that the question is not a characteristic of maturity.

Our culture is of no help to us in regard to patience. Technology has reduced the wait time for computers, shopping, information gathering, and much more. Instant access to food, cash, and answers has conditioned us to instant expectations. We therefore expect quicker progression toward healing and restoration.

Nevertheless, we wonder where we are in the journey that has placed us in what seems to be a godforsaken desert. Though patience is a virtue and perseverance is a quality of great worth—and though we need to be receptive to the development of those qualities in our lives—there are some mile–markers that offer us some perspective on where we might be in our journey. These *mile–markers* (my term) have been identified through the extensive research of Rory Remer and Robert A. Ferguson in their article "Becoming a Secondary Survivor of Sexual Assault."[30]

## EXPLORING A NEW PERSPECTIVE

Remer and Ferguson identified six mile–markers or stages through which couples pass on their journey from trauma to healing. Two things were observed about these couples who were traveling a road in marriage just like you and me.

> **Remer and Ferguson identified six mile–markers or stages through which couples pass on their journey from trauma to healing.**

First, there was an inter–connectedness: the husband mirrored his wife's experience and vice versa. When a wife who was a survivor of childhood sexual abuse experienced trauma through a nightmare or flashback, her husband experienced some degree of trauma as well. Similarly, when a wife progressed towards healing, her husband was also likely to make progress. But the wife's healing also relied on the progressive healing of her husband. As distant as you might feel from your wife, or she from you, couples tend to travel through the stages of trauma and healing together.

Second, the experience of the couples in the study indicated six-mile markers along this pathway through which we travel from trauma towards healing. Using the markers Remer and Ferguson identified in their research, let's examine the experiences of men I interviewed in my own research.

### Marker #1: Pre-Trauma Stage

The pre-trauma stage occurs prior to the survivor's disclosure of abuse or prior to the time when the survivor can no longer push the reality of the abuse into her subconscious. It is a period of turmoil, often an ambiguous turmoil. In my own experience, a perturbing darkness and sense of hopelessness began plaguing my wife for the first time in her adult years. Her bright countenance was slowly disappearing. I mirrored her trauma with my own confusion.

When I interviewed Bryan, a husband of a survivor, I asked what it was that prompted his wife's disclosure of her childhood sexual abuse. He answered, "She wasn't prepared to tell me. I caught it. And, I asked her point blank, 'Were you molested?' I recognized what I saw."

Bryan went on to explain what he recognized.

> I was also molested as a child from twelve to fifteen by a family member. I recognized the frustration, shame, anger, and sadness that all go with childhood sexual abuse. It was fairly easy for me to recognize my own feelings in her.

For Bryan, the pre-trauma was recognizing his own abuse through his wife. For his wife, her pre-trauma stage consisted of experiencing some effects of her abuse without yet acknowledging to herself the reality of the abuse.

The pathway from trauma to healing is not a direct route. Throughout the process, and at any time, we circle back to earlier mile markers. This was the experience for Wes. His wife was thrown back into the pre-trauma stage when she had additional recall of her abuse. Wes described one incident.

> *I remember once we were traveling to another state and she started doing this finger [fidgety] thing. I could tell, "Oh, here we go." She maybe sometimes would start crying or whatever. I said, "What's going on?" She said, "I remember something about a motorcycle and ah, the woods..." It went on for a few minutes... A lot of times, those things happened right when she was on the edge of sleep, right when she was dozing off... She was dozing off and she just got this uneasy feeling and this fragment of a memory happened.*

Sometimes we don't know that we are in the pre–trauma stage until we come to the next mile marker.

## Marker #2: Trauma Awareness

The trauma awareness stage is subsequent to the survivor's disclosure of her childhood sexual abuse. During this stage, the survivor begins recognizing the effects of the trauma and the abnormality she is experiencing. She may begin speculating their link to her childhood sexual abuse.

Wes offered a vivid example of his trauma awareness as he described an occasion when his wife's nightmare depicted everything that had happened to her in one incident of her childhood sexual abuse. When she awoke in a disturbed state, Wes got a notebook and instructed her to record what she had just experienced. Wes described what happened.

> *When I turned and looked at her it was probably the most shocking turning point and experience because I saw her grasping the pen as though in a little kid's hand and trying to, in little kid's handwriting, write what was happening to her. It was in the vocabulary of a little kid. It just rocked me because I didn't think that was possible.*[31]

Wes's trauma awareness was exposed by his description of the event as "shocking." His wife's trauma awareness was obvious.

Another example would be in how a survivor's anger toward her past or her perpetrator is expressed. An intensified anger with more vivid expressions of rage can depict trauma awareness. The survivor's husband, being the recipient or observer of the rage, also becomes aware of the trauma.

### Marker #3: Crisis And Disorientation

The effects of childhood sexual abuse include but are not limited to depression, anxiety, panic attacks, shame, nightmares, paralyzing fear, flashbacks, life–dominating distrust of people, and sexual aversion or sexual perversion. Some effects were developed as coping strategies such as dissociation, withdrawal, and spending sprees. The effects and the coping strategies, though they might lie latent for a time, eventually emerge to fuel crisis and disorientation.

Our words and communications can give evidence of our crisis and disorientation. Crisis and disorientation is indicated when a husband wonders "What just happened?" or "What is happening?"

Bryan indicated his crisis and disorientation when he recounted his conversations with Mandy regarding their lack of sexual intimacy. He said,

> *I start off with the best of intentions, and it seems somehow to always flip over on me and become my issue, not hers. This is really confusing. There's days I walk into the conversations, I'm like, "Ok, how did that happen?"*

The sexual relationship can be a context for this stage in the journey. Crisis and disorientation is starkly evident when the survivor of abuse confuses the present sexual intimacy of love and trust with the past sexual injury of violation and hurt.

Dan, another husband of a survivor of childhood sexual abuse, captured the frustration inherent in the crisis and disorientation. He said,

> *I couldn't fix it—couldn't do anything about it… I can't process this. I either want to go cry because I'm so sad that it happened and she has to deal with this, or, since I know the perpetrator, I want to shoot him.*

We are now ready to consider the final three stages of the pathway towards healing. Markers four through six move us from the experience of trauma—highlighted in markers one through three—to the desired goal of healing.

### Marker #4: Outward Adjustment: Personal and Relational

Our attempts to return to the status quo, or what we view as being *normal* for our marriage, indicate that we've entered into the adjustment stage.

In other words, the adjustment stage begins with our efforts to restore the patterns and expectations that characterized the pre–trauma stage of our marriage relationship. In this stage, we ask questions like, "Why can't we [name your activity] like we used to?"

Caution is warranted in our attempt to return to life as it was before the pre–trauma stage. No doubt, there may have been many happy times in the pre–trauma years. That was certainly the case for me, and I hope it will be so for you too. For my wife and me, those were the years when our daughters were born and raised. I can make a long list of phenomenal memories.

However, the desire to return to the pre–trauma stage is likely based on some inaccurate or incomplete perceptions. We are probably assuming that our relationship with our wives was at a higher level of emotional health than was actually the case. And perhaps we're also assuming that our own emotional state was healthier than it might have actually been. Oh, I thought I was fine back in those years. But I know better now.

Another outward adjustment is our effort to offer greater support for our wives. The emotional injury that occurs to survivors from childhood sexual abuse compromises any ability they did have to offer emotional support. I was blessed, and so were my daughters, to have received emotional support from my wife during the pre–trauma years. I know that is not the case for many husbands. But once we are in the trauma awareness stage, our wives' ability to extend themselves to us is thwarted. A husband who previously received emotional support from his wife needs to adjust by offering more emotional support to her.

I have observed some husbands, ones who are inclined towards fixing things in the relationship, offer their version of emotional support and encouragement in a way that is dominating or controlling. This must be guarded against.

A commonly used metaphor by husbands of childhood sexual abuse survivors is that they feel as though they are "walking on eggshells." This feeling might be especially true during the two stages of disorientation and adjustment. Typical statements from husbands during this time are, "I can't say or do anything right." Clint used the eggshell metaphor and continued saying that he was "clueless as to what to do. I'm walking so gently. I don't want to say anything that will upset her. I don't want to push the wrong buttons."

The adjustments of this stage are outward and can be awkward as couples attempt to find a new normal. Inward adjustments begin with the next mile–marker.

**Marker #5: Reorganization: Personal and Relational**

Self–awareness is the prerequisite to crossing the mile–marker into the stage of reorganization. Once we are self–aware, we can identify the unhealthy values, attitudes, and behavioral patterns that characterized our lives prior to and during the pre–trauma stage. By acknowledging the unhealthy and dysfunctional attributes, we can then do some reorganizing of our lives. Wes referred to his own experience in the reorganization stage as "reconstruction." In this stage, Wes revisited previously held assumptions saying,

> ... *things you thought were fact... now what do you do? Well, you've got to reconstruct something... The foundation that you built on was not built on facts, but now we're putting the facts, we're putting the building blocks back in place.*

When I interviewed Chad, he gave witness to how he reorganized his attitude and expression of love by saying, "It doesn't matter what she says or how hurtful things that were said could be. I'm going to love her unconditionally." Referring to his pre–trauma stage and earlier, Chad said, "I was a failure early on. I didn't know the things I know now. I didn't know how to love unconditionally." Though Chad indicated that Barb's effects from childhood sexual abuse had ceased, he spoke more of how he was different than how she was different.

> **Though Chad indicated that Barb's effects from childhood sexual abuse had ceased, he spoke more of how he was different than how she was different.**

Dan spoke about the reorganization that occurred for him in regard to his sexual relationship with his wife, Nikki. After describing how he watched her pain and listened to her at length as she poured out the toxin, Dan then began to experience a change within him.

*My heart began to change with it. And, so, for me, I began not just to desire her, and not desire like sex, but more like intimacy. [I realized] there's a purpose for sex other than me having an orgasm; it's oneness in our marriage—a great bond. And, when I started to pursue her that way. Man! That was a big shift in our marriage.*

Reorganization creates a safer environment in the relationship. The safer environment opens the door for possible further disclosure that then re-routes the couple back to the trauma awareness stage. This time, however, the trauma can be faced with deeper understanding and a higher level of emotional health.

The reorganization stage reveals that healing usually involves a tremendous amount of unlearning and relearning. The hard work must be done individually as both husband and wife work through their individual dysfunctions and then join together in facing the problems in their couple relationship.

> **The reorganization stage reveals that healing usually involves a tremendous amount of unlearning and relearning.**

In my own experience, reorganization or reconstruction would not have occurred without professional counseling. The depth of self-awareness and self-discovery that were necessary for me to own up to my dysfunctions and to develop new patterns could only come by way of the wise guidance from a competent counselor.

### Marker #6: Integration and Resolution

For husbands, integration refers to accepting the trauma by accepting our wives and ourselves for who we have become. I believe that it was C. S Lewis who referred to our lives as being like the rings in a tree. The inner rings–all the experiences of previous years–cannot be removed. They are and always will be part of our story. But none of our previous experiences are the whole story. Trauma will always be part of our story, but it is not our whole story. We have grown and matured beyond the "rings of trauma."

**Trauma will always be part of our story,
but it is not our whole story.**

Resolution does not refer to everything being resolved, but rather to an appreciation of the healing that has occurred and the ever–continuing healing yet to occur. Once this stage is reached, new memories or disclosures do not throw a couple back into disorientation. Instead, they return to reorganization, taking a route that is more effectively and efficiently navigated.

## Mile-Markers in the Journey Towards Healing

*1. Pre-Trauma Stage*
*2. Trauma Awareness*
*3. Crisis and Disorientation*
*4. Outward Adjustment: Personal and Relational*
*5. Reorganization: Personal and Relational*
*6. Integration and Resolution*

Experience with couples affected by childhood sexual abuse consistently shows that professional counseling is necessary for healing to occur in the survivor of the abuse. Counseling is also necessary for husbands of survivors in order to prevent dysfunctional patterns such as codependency.

This journey is not traveled in a straight line. Sometimes we circle back to previous mile markers. But these markers can help us see more clearly where we are currently walking in the path of healing.

### ESTABLISHING NEW PATTERNS

"When will this be over?" Questions like this are counterproductive. First of all, survivors do not have the answer to the question. More importantly, the question hinders their process of healing by prompting them to conclude, "If this is not good for him, then it is not safe for me. So I'll shut down."

The question implies impatient waiting. "How long do I have to wait for this to be over?" My challenge to you is to shift your perspective from *waiting* to *wading*.

**My challenge to you is to shift
your perspective from waiting to wading.**

*Wading* means "to walk in or through water or something else that similarly impedes normal movement."[32] This serves as a meaningful metaphor for the journey of a survivor and her husband. There are two qualities necessary for successful wading. First, steadiness is necessary in order to maintain consistency in progressing against the resistance. Second, resilience is necessary so that we might bounce back from any setbacks brought on by the more powerful current or waves that work against us.

Our steady and resilient wading through the journey establishes a much different attitude than waiting through the journey. Waiting implies "hurry up" as opposed to steady resilience. As already indicated, an impatience in waiting communicates to our wives that they are not performing well enough, which thwarts any sense of safety that they might experience. On the other hand, our perspective and conduct of steady resilience in wading creates a safe environment for our wives, which is a quality of life that they most value.

**...our perspective and conduct of steady resilience
in wading creates a safe environment for our wives,
which is a quality of life that they most value.**

As we will see in Chapter 6, husbands of survivors are also subject to trauma during the journey, giving them the designation of *secondary survivor*. So the question here becomes, "How can I be steady when I am traumatized too?" The answer to that question is to develop patterns in our own self-care.

For many years, I ignorantly assumed that any word prefixed with "self" depicted a lack of virtue: selfish, self-indulgent, self-righteous, self-pity. I've now awakened to the fact that there are many exceptions, and self-care is one of those exceptions. Jesus, the personification of self*less*ness and knowing the limitations of his followers, guided them in self-care. When "so many people were coming and going that they did not even have a chance to eat, he said to them, 'Come with me by yourselves to a quiet place and get some rest (Mark 6:31).'"

Self-care must be a non-negotiable for husbands whose wives are survivors of childhood sexual abuse. We face unique and demanding challenges. We also have our limitations physically, emotionally, and spiritually.

So what does self–care mean for us? Here are sensible guidelines that have helped me for many years. I believe that if we don't engage in these practices now, a toll will be taken on our lives, our wives, and our families.

### 1. Know Your Limits

Some husbands take on the role of the therapist, but I've yet to meet a couple who are doing well when the husband has assumed that self–appointed role. Sharon E. Cheston wisely stated, "Do not underestimate your input and do not overestimate your skills."[33] Self–care means that we take the pressure off ourselves to figure out the pathway of healing for our wives.

Are we to intervene if they seek to bring harm to themselves? Yes! Are we to interject what we think is going on in their minds? No! Instead, do all you can to support your wife in finding a good therapist.

### 2. Draw Lines of Responsibility

In marriage, there is a degree to which each person identifies with the other. In the past, I thought "the more identified I am with my wife the better." I did not realize at the time how unhealthy it was—and how unhealthy I was. I became so enmeshed or entwined with my wife that I lost a sense of who I was and what my own needs were. My self–awareness occurred only at times when I groveled in self-pity. That's why my counselor had to work with me in order for me to discover *"What's it like to be Bill?"*

> **Self-care means that we take the pressure off ourselves to figure out the pathway of healing for our wives.**

One way that enmeshment occurs is when a husband ignores his own needs and seeks only to satisfy the needs of his wife. That's what I was doing. And I thought it was healthy and loving to do so. My wife, however, felt smothered. I could not even say what restaurant I wanted to eat at. I would force her to make her choice because I wanted to make sure she was pleased. I was treating her as a child. I was not giving her the benefit of the doubt that she was not a child, even though there were times when, because of the abuse, it was the damaged child who was visible.

The enmeshment kept me from ever revealing what I liked or disliked. In other words, the enmeshment kept me from revealing me, the one whom she was longing to know. You can read more about this in Chapter 9.

Intimacy is knowing and being known. Enmeshment kept me from being known. I needed to take responsibility for being known by identifying me and revealing me to my wife.

I also had to learn the matters for which I was not responsible. Husbands of survivors become enmeshed with their wives when they feel as though they are at fault for their wife's struggles. This is especially true when we are the recipient of her inner rage or outer distancing.

My counselor, Dr. Daniel Green, kept reminding me that I am responsible for two things. I'm responsible for how I treat myself, and I'm responsible for how I treat others—no more than that, no less than that. I am not responsible for (a) how others treat me, (b) how others treat others, or (c) how others treat themselves.[34] Therefore, self–care means setting boundaries of responsibility, knowing that I am not responsible for her childhood sexual abuse or for her response to it.

### 3. Don't Shut Off Your Feelings

The perversion of sexuality that heaped shame on our wives can result in an infrequency of intimacy that heaps shame on us. This feeling and experience of shame disconnects us not only from our wives but also from other husbands. In our embarrassment, we will not take the risk of joining any men's group that discusses marriage. If sexual intimacy is discussed, what will we say if our own experience of intimacy seems to occur as infrequently as the Bears winning the Super Bowl? We therefore isolate ourselves and compartmentalize our feelings in a box that we try to keep shut. We attempt to disconnect ourselves from the hurt and anger—feelings—and consequently disconnect from others—people. This disconnection is shame, it is hiding from being fully known.

Self–care does not mean that husbands shut down by not feeling. Self–care means that the healthy thing for husbands is to get counseling for themselves. Self–care recognizes our personal coping limitations and willingly seeks out a counselor who can be our competent confidant.

### 4. Do What You Love to Do

What do you enjoy doing? What activity brings a feeling of "I'm glad I did that!" to your heart? Some husbands of survivors have been addressing the needs of their wives for so long that they cannot remember the last time they relaxed and had some fun.

What do you enjoy doing, and when is the last time you've done it? In case it's been a long time since you did what you love doing, here's a list of possible stress relievers:

- Golf (not on my personal list)
- Fishing (Nope! Not that either)
- Hiking
- Motorcycling
- Cards
- Reading
- Community recreational leagues
- Movies
- Skeet shooting
- Cooking
- Photography
- Model building

I'm suggesting that you establish some agreement with your wife and that you take time, individually, to engage in some healthy activity on a regular basis that will offer fun and replenishment. It is necessary for your own individual growth and the health of your marriage that you express your own needs.

For some of you, I know that expressing your needs to your wife is an intimidating idea. From my conversations with husbands, I know that some fear hearing something like this from their wives: "What? You are concerned about your needs? So tell me, how have you suffered?" It's tough to receive a response like that. If that happens to you, it's time to go back and draw lines of responsibility. It is ironic that men, who are taught to be tough, can have difficulty expressing their own needs. Dr. Noelle Wiersma has done some terrific work on this matter of expressing ourselves in marriages affected by childhood sexual abuse. I discuss this in Chapter 9.

**Self-care means regularly engaging in activities
that are appropriate morally, healthy physically,
and replenishing emotionally.**

For now, being faithful in your marriage does not mean being negligent to your own needs—those come with being human. Self-care means regularly engaging in activities that are appropriate morally, healthy physically, and replenishing emotionally.

### 5. Daily Time with God

I know this may sound really odd—maybe weird—to you if you don't share the same spiritual beliefs I do. But please hear me out.

Countless times, I've told God everything that was going on. Even though He already knew what was going on, I believe He listened. There have been other times when I've vented my frustration to Him. I believe He listened then too, but He also pierced my thoughts with His response. I remember crying out to God in pain for how marriages affected by childhood sexual abuse have to endure times when the survivor seems so distant. God responded, "I totally understand," and I knew He did understand because there have been times when I've been the one distant from Him.

There's not an event, attitude, or behavior that God has not already experienced Himself. I've yet to think of one. Because of His identification with us, He has told us, "We don't have a priest who is out of touch with our reality. He's been through weakness and testing, experienced it all—all but the sin. So let's walk right up to him and get what he is so ready to give. Take the mercy, accept the help (Hebrews 4:15–15, The Message)."

We also need the daily intake of His Word as it is given to us in the scriptures. Don't read for information. Read to know God. Don't race through His message. Read slowly and listen carefully. To be in His presence is to receive the best self-care available.

## CONCLUSION

We've noted from the work of Remer and Ferguson that we, as husbands, walk alongside our wives whether we choose to or not. We are experiencing a mirrored version of their trauma and disorientation. It is a journey. It has unexpected twists and turns, and it loops around, sometimes appearing to take us backward.

But there can be more to our mirrored journey with our wives. As husbands of childhood sexual abuse survivors, our compassion and care for our wives are acts of partnership with God. God walks among the weary and brokenhearted. "The Lord is close to the brokenhearted and saves those who are crushed in spirit (Psalm 34:18)"

To love and care for our wives is to join God in His work. For some sovereign reason, God has selected you, me, and other husbands of survivors to be a conduit of His love and care for our wives. As He imparts some of His care through us, He has also promised to extend His care to us. We can trust Him to replenish us because He has said, "I will refresh the weary and satisfy the faint (Jeremiah 31:25)." That's the best way to experience self-care.

**God walks among the weary and brokenhearted.**

## Chapter Five: Personal Application

1. Determine how and where your observations of and experiences in your marriage fit into Remer and Ferguson's stages of the journey from pre–trauma to integration and resolution.

2. Google and print a list of feelings. Here's a possible link: http://www.psychpage.com/learning/library/assess/feelings.html

    a. What feelings have you acknowledged?

    b. What feelings have you not acknowledged?

3. What healthy steps will you take to acknowledge your feelings?

4. Make of list of activities that are appropriate morally, healthy physically, and replenishing emotionally for you. Schedule and engage in the activity.

For a more in-depth review of this chapter, we have also provided a full, free downloadable "Guide for Application" on our website: www.marriagereconstructionministries.org.
It is our hope that the additional questions in this guide will take you further into potential personal and marital growth.

Chapter Six

# WHY CAN'T SHE JUST GET OVER IT?

In my previous chapter, "When Will This Be Over?" the word "this" in the question referred to the undesirable and disruptive experiences that arise as outcomes of childhood sexual abuse within a marriage relationship.

Another question asked by many frustrated husbands of survivors is "Why can't she just get over it?" This question may seem similar, but it is a different question because it points towards a person rather than a circumstance. The first question could be modified to "When will this depression be over for my wife?" The question for this chapter is more biting since it could be modified to "Why can't my wife just get over her depression?" In the first question, a husband reveals his frustration with the experience or circumstance. In the question that we are now considering, a husband is expressing his frustration more directly with his wife. The first question assumes that nothing can be done to control the timing of when "this" will be over. The current question, on the other hand, assumes that a survivor of childhood sexual abuse can do something, and therefore she should be able to take control of her despair.

Some husbands would be insensitively direct in asking their wives when they will get over whatever symptomology is most affecting their relationship. Other husbands would not ask their wives but would inquire of a counselor, "When will she get over this?" Then there are many husbands who express their frustration in other forms of statements, questions, or moods.

On more occasions than I want to admit, I was insensitive to my wife's hard–fought battles. I was most often thoughtless when an effect of her abuse would resurface after a sustained time of reprieve. I would be instantly disheartened, and I turned my angst towards her by saying, "This again?" She knew it was pointed at her. She felt my assumption and expectation that she should be over it. I regret those times.

Quincy acknowledged his resentment towards Randi. He wondered when she would get over her depression and eating disorders. He was irritated that her counseling was costing money. His question of Randi was,

*Why aren't things better now? Why do you need to keep going back and picking the scab?*

Nelson spoke of Jan's ability to pour herself into her work, her enthusiasm in singing on their church's worship team, and how she could be so absorbed in other things, but "when it comes to us, it's like… there's elements when she'll get over it or set it aside or whatever and we can be good for a while… and then it slips back in, six, eight weeks later or something."

Roger's wife, Beth, was involved in an extramarital affair; the affair was one aspect of her promiscuous lifestyle that seemed to stem from her childhood sexual abuse. Beth confessed all in an email to Roger. After things seemed to have settled, he took the email and burned it. It was a ceremonial act of putting her deception behind. He told Beth, "I'm setting this behind me, and I'm telling you right now I'm never bringing this up again." He kept his word and never used it against her.

But in a very strange way, Beth could not move beyond her past. Though Roger did not use her past against her, she used it. Roger said,

*In an argument, she's actually used it two or three times in the last year. So that was weird to me. I don't know, I don't know if that's still the guilt there. Fact is, it caused one of our arguments a couple of weeks ago. I said, "Are you over all that? You know, maybe you aren't over it? Yeah, I mean, I'm over it. I don't bring it up. You bring it up. Maybe you aren't over it."*

There are multiple motives as to why husbands ask, "Why can't she just get over it?" There can be a selfless motive of a man sincerely wishing that his wife could be freed of the pain. There can also be a selfish motive of a man no longer wanting his life and comfort to be interrupted with the pain. Have you identified your motive in asking the question?

**There are multiple motives as to why husbands ask, "Why can't she just get over it?"**

Addressing the question of "Why can't she just get over it?" requires understanding of our wife's situation. Simply put, to address this question appropriately, we must place our self in our wife's shoes empathetically. Let's begin exploring.

## EXPLORING A NEW PERSPECTIVE

A procedure in horse breeding offers a vivid analogy of the imprint inflicted upon the soul of the childhood sexual abuse survivor. Les Sellnow, in his article "Foal Imprinting," explains that when a mare goes into labor and gives birth, the foal initially lies helpless in the straw or on the grass. The human handler quietly approaches the wet foal that is drawing its first breaths. The handler kneels beside the foal, begins toweling the newborn dry, runs his or her gentle hands over its body, and repeats the motion until there is no longer a response.

The goal is desensitization. The desensitization is accomplished through a gradual process wherein the handler eliminates the response of the foal to the stimulus. This process of rubbing and touching is called *imprinting*. When done successfully, the foal will eventually yield to being saddled, muzzled, and even to bodily invasions that occur for medical purposes.[35]

Perpetrators of childhood sexual abuse are human handlers of a very different sort. The intentional, intrusive, and insidious actions by these perpetrator "handlers" upon young girls results in an imprint that compromises responses, muzzles any outcry, and suffers appalling and unwanted invasions.

**The intentional, intrusive, and insidious actions by these perpetrator "handlers" upon young girls results in an imprint that compromises responses, muzzles any outcry, and suffers appalling and unwanted invasions.**

Childhood sexual abuse inflicts an imprint that conditions the survivor with responses and nonresponses as though they have been inbred. The imprint penetrates deep into the survivor's soul and permeates broadly through the survivor's affect (emotion), behavior, and cognition (knowledge and beliefs). The notion that survivors can "just get over it" ignores the depth and breadth of the imprint.

The long-term impact of the imprint is evidence of the traumatic nature of the abuse. During the 1970s, research and clinical practice began recognizing the long-term effects of childhood sexual abuse, phenomena that had been set aside and ignored since the 1890s. Further research in the 1990s indicated that childhood sexual abuse resulted in symptoms similar to those experienced by Vietnam war veterans who experienced war-related trauma.[36] Consequently, sexual abuse became recognized as a traumatic event for the victim. Today, post-traumatic stress disorder (PTSD) is a recognized diagnosis among clinicians of many survivors of childhood sexual abuse. Abuse situations involving incest have the greatest risk for traumatization due to the close relation and its duration.

Further study has led to the realization that the trauma for the survivor of childhood sexual abuse extends even further than the designation of PTSD and has led to the designation of Complex Trauma. Heather Davediuk Gingrich offers an insightful work on Complex Trauma in her book *Restoring the Shattered Self: A Christian Counselor's Guide to Complex Trauma*. One example of Complex Trauma's distinction from PTSD is the nature of the one who inflicts the trauma. A war veteran experiences PTSD as a result of the trauma inflicted by an enemy. On the other hand, a survivor of childhood sexual abuse experiences PTSD as a result, in many cases, of the trauma that was inflicted by a loved one or family friend, not a perceived enemy. The conundrum of being abused by someone who is supposed to care presents a complexity unknown in most other traumas.[37]

The notion that survivors can "just get over it" ignores the trauma of abuse and the intricately intertwined wiring of our personhood: emotional, sexual, mental, and physical. Complex Trauma complicates the recovery even further.

Appendix A shows the full diagnostic criterion for post-traumatic stress disorder from the *Diagnostic and Statistical Manual for Mental Disorders* (DSM-5).[38] My abbreviated description here includes brief explanations of how the criterion can be experienced in childhood sexual abuse.

**Intrusive Thoughts with Physical Effects:** Trauma affects both body and mind. For example, the body responds to subsequent triggers of previous trauma. For the survivor of childhood sexual abuse, intrusive recollection can occur through nightmares and flashbacks of the childhood sexual abuse. Rational thought does not thwart the response. The body and mind react as though the past traumatic events are occurring in the present. The symptoms include accelerated heart rate, cold sweats, heart palpitations, and hyper–startle responses. Sexually intrusive thoughts were noted in a study that investigated whether women with a history of childhood sexual abuse had different sexual fantasies from women with no childhood sexual abuse. The study's 138 participants ranged in age from 18 to 41. The findings indicated the intrusive nature of the fantasies for women with a history of childhood sexual abuse and that "they had more fantasies with the theme of being under someone else's control."[39]

**Avoidant/Numbing:** Stacie Putnam, a survivor of childhood sexual abuse, speaks of a survivor's sense that *the monster that was once in her bed had been replaced by the monster in her head.*[40] Who would not want to be numb from that torture?

Those who suffer from PTSD from childhood sexual abuse avoid situations, thoughts, and feelings that are associated with the traumatic event. Emotional numbing, dissociation, and shame are common among survivors. Therapists hear common expressions from survivors, such as "It's too dangerous for me to let my wall down," "I will never trust him," and "I am damaged and unlovable."[41] Survivors of childhood sexual abuse usually prefer to avoid intimacy, communication involving emotions, and circumstances and conversations in which there is lack of control.

**Hyper–Arousal:** As noted in the Criterion for PTSD, persistent symptoms of increasing arousal (not present before the trauma) are indicated by at least two of the following: (1) difficulty falling or staying asleep, (2) irritability or outbursts of anger, (3) difficulty concentrating, (4) hyper–vigilance, (5) reckless or self–destructive behavior, and (6) exaggerated startle response. For example, a survivor whose daughter becomes the age that the survivor was when abused will not only be alert to the possibility of her daughter encountering abuse, but will constantly be "reading" expressions, gestures, moods, and actions of her daughter and those around her on high–alert.

**Summarization:** The PTSD diagnosis illuminates the broad and deep impact that childhood sexual abuse can have on a marriage relationship. Trauma inflicted by one person on another, as occurs in childhood sexual abuse, provokes symptoms affecting daily functioning, damages the building blocks of relationships such as trust and security, and renders the partner of the traumatized person feeling helpless and hopeless. The survivor's body and mind react as though the past traumatic events are occurring in the present.

These effects from the trauma of childhood sexual abuse have a trajectory into marriage and other close relationships. "'Trauma victims' marriages are, therefore, more likely to become distressed and once distressed tend to become stuck in particularly intense self–perpetuating cycles of distance, defense, and distrust."[42]

Husbands of survivors who recognize the imprint and trauma inflicted upon their wives as a result of childhood sexual abuse can adopt a new and healthier perspective. Understanding the nature of the imprint and of PTSD, husbands can recognize that the long–term effects are not something that a survivor can "just get over." In the same way that we would never tell a war veteran to "just get over it," so it should be in regard to the survivor of sexual abuse. But with good counsel and hard work on the part of the survivor, God can handcraft His own redemptive imprint on the survivor. Furthermore, as only God can do, He can use the trauma to refine rather than define the survivor's life. God's redemptive imprint and refining is all in His timing and in His way.

> **Understanding the nature of the imprint and of PTSD, husbands can recognize that the long–term effects are not something that a survivor can "just get over."**

In light of this new perspective, how might we as husbands respond? What patterns can we adopt that will enable us to live as emotionally healthy men and husbands?

## ESTABLISHING NEW PATTERNS

This first step may surprise you. But it is a necessary step toward reality— and healthy thinking cannot occur without accepting reality.

### 1. Recognize Your Own Trauma

My interviews with husbands whose wives are survivors of childhood sexual abuse consistently revealed that trauma is not isolated within their wives. Being exposed to the effects of childhood sexual abuse can be traumatic.

Consequently, husbands of childhood sexual abuse survivors are often referred to as "secondary survivors" or "secondary victims." Close family members can experience a "secondary trauma" due to their close proximity to and care for the survivor.

You might relate to Chad, whose wife, Barb, became a "non–functioning wife... almost overnight." Chad described his secondary trauma by saying,

> *She was listless... She wanted to sleep all day... I'd have to physically pick her up out of the bed, stand her up,... I'd walk her into the shower, turn on the shower...*

Barb's effects from her childhood sexual abuse included isolation and lack of interest in their daughters. Chad recalled, "She started talking about moving out and getting away from all of it. She didn't want the girls. And she wanted a new life." Another husband, Nate, came in the house after being out one night and described how he found Jamie.

> *I came in the bedroom. She was curled up next to her bed in the corner of the room, shaking, convulsing. And then she just confessed to me all kinds of stuff no guy wants to ever hear. She confessed to me the child abuse. She confessed to me an affair. She confessed to me promiscuous stuff before we were married that I didn't know about. She let it out. And I just, all I could do was hold her. She goes, "You hate me. I'll pack up. I'll leave."*

You may recall how Wes described his world as being rocked when he observed Jyl's journaling after a nightmare about her childhood sexual abuse.

> *When I turned and looked at her, that was probably the most shocking turning point in my experience because I saw her grasping at the pen as in a little kid's hand and, ah, trying to in printed little kid's handwriting write what was happening to her... It was in, ah, the vocabulary of a little kid... it just rocked me because I didn't think that was possible.*

This phenomenon is known as Dissociative Identity Disorder (DID) and is addressed in Chapter 10.

Wade's wife experienced a less common effect that has been associated with childhood sexual abuse by living under the threat of his wife's potential criminal activity. Shoplifting has been noted as a possible behavioral outcome of childhood sexual abuse. Wade's wife, Tina, had a clean criminal record. However, she came home on multiple occasions with merchandise that she had not purchased. Wade reported feeling traumatized himself as he contemplated that someday he might be called to the local police station in their small town, where everybody seems to know everybody and their business, to visit his wife behind bars.

Chad's attempt to get Barb out of bed when she was listless, Nate's bedroom encounter with Jamie, Wes's startling observation of Jyl's re-entrance into her childhood, and Wade's fearful anticipation of an eventual phone call from the local police were occasions in which the husbands perceived that they entered into their own trauma.

Recognizing our own trauma is not for the purpose of casting us into fear and emotional paralysis. Rather, our recognition of our own sense of trauma prevents us from living in denial so that we can manage ourselves.

Our need to manage ourselves leads us to the second step of living in the context of our wife's trauma while we deal with our own trauma.

## 2. Revisit and Realize Your Assumptions

Most of the husbands of childhood sexual abuse survivors that I have met can be placed in two categories: (a) those who were unsuspecting and learned of their wife's abuse several years into their marriage and (b) those who married knowing about their wife's past but assumed the abuse had little or no effect on their relationship. In both cases, husbands must "accept that there never was a time when the couple was unaffected by the trauma history, even at the outset of their relationship, when the event may not have been fully remembered."[43] Remember the imprint that has occurred on your wife. The sexual violation of childhood sexual abuse is a unique trauma in that it invades and injures a young girl's psyche, piling intense shame upon her. There is no way that this abuse *cannot* affect subsequent relationships, especially intimate relationships. To assume that abuse of the past does not have affect in the present is denial of reality. Accordingly, to assume that trauma of the past will not impose trauma in the present is also denial of reality.

A competent counselor for a survivor of childhood sexual abuse will guide her in accepting what she wishes she could deny—the reality of the abuse—and acknowledging how it is affecting her in the present. Without this acceptance and acknowledgment, she lives in a world of false assumptions. The counselor will seek to expel these false assumptions and adopt healthier feeling, thinking, and acting.

Likewise, the husband of a survivor must expel the false assumption that he is not and has not been affected by his wife's trauma history.

### 3. Recalculate How to Navigate

The effects of childhood sexual abuse exhibit an extreme nature. For example, most people experience shame at various points and to various degrees. For the survivor, however, the experience of shame is more intense, more constant, and more detrimental to their relationships and daily functioning.

The effects can also exist as polar opposites from one survivor to the next. For example, one survivor of childhood sexual abuse may have sexual preoccupations and exhibit promiscuous behavior while another may exhibit aversions to any sexual contact. Another example is that one survivor might display aggression while another shows detachment. Some survivors are extremely dependent while others are controlling.

The extreme and polarized nature of childhood sexual abuse's effects present unique and sometimes unnerving challenges to husbands. One husband might be afraid to come home from work for fear of his wife's anger and aggression. Another husband may be afraid to leave for work due to his wife's vulnerable state and suicidal tendency. Learning to navigate through life can become a 24/7 preoccupation for the husband.

It can be tempting for husbands to distance themselves as a means of self-protection from the emotional pain. I've observed some husbands who distance themselves physically by taking on as much business travel as possible. Others might distance themselves *emotionally* through numbing.

There is no easy route when seeking how to navigate through such diverse and trauma-inducing scenarios. A general guideline, however, is to *serve as an anchor: be steady and soothing.*

I asked Nate how he responded when he found Jamie curled up and convulsing in the corner of the room. He responded, "I held her. I said, '...

We'll work through this.'" Wes described his world as being "rocked" when he saw Jyl writing like a child. Nevertheless, he remained calm in that moment so as not to further startle her.

I have had occasions in the past when I was scared like never before and feared for my wife's safety. Here's what I recommend in order to remain steady and navigate through the trauma:

*A. Identify What You Are Thinking, Feeling, and Doing.*

My *modus operandi*, too often, is to think in terms of "how am I being affected?" As I write this, in a more objective state of thought, I am thinking, "My goodness! Isn't the bigger issue 'How is my wife being affected?'"

Actually, it should be a combination. We should think of our wives. The effects of childhood sexual abuse upon them are brutal. Many of us are fortunate enough to have wives who fight to survive. Their battles result from an imprint that was inflicted upon them as an innocent child. In every way, it is outrageous that the abuse ever happened.

But we must also be mindful of how we are being affected. I'm not simply referring to how we've been inconvenienced. There are many events in life that inconvenience us: slow traffic, cancelled flights, delayed projects, and so on. Being inconvenienced is part of life. I'm referring to how our thoughts or perspectives are being impacted by the trauma we are facing. Are we becoming bitter? Hopeless? Are our questions to God transitioning more to accusations towards God?

We men can be so good at compartmentalizing our thoughts. But when trauma like this gets stuffed into a compartment, it festers and infiltrates into other dimensions of our life, such as high blood pressure, sleeplessness, or other physical maladies.

Dr. Daniel Green says, "When we name it, we tame it." Identifying and acknowledging our thoughts, especially to a trusted friend, can tame its power.

We also need to identify what we are feeling. What some refer to as the SASHET has been helpful to me. It is an acronym for our emotions. Am I *S*ad, *A*ngry, *S*cared, *H*appy, *E*xcited, or *T*ender (or a combination of 2 or 3)? *Tender* might refer to deep feelings about what someone else is experiencing, or it can refer to my own fragile feelings about what I am experiencing.

There's a qualification with the SASHET. Many of us men would want to say, "I'm a little angry." But the word "little" is not allowed in the SASHET. If we sense we are a little angry, then *we are angry*.

The SASHET not only identifies, it distinguishes. Fear and anger can so often overlap. I got angry one time because a dog owner allowed her German Shepherd to run loose one afternoon in our neighborhood. This dog had not been to obedience school. When the dog growled at me and showed its teeth—I was on a public sidewalk—I got really mad and yelled back at the dog. As I reflected later on the incident, I realized that I was more scared than angry.

There have been so many times when dealing with the trauma of childhood sexual abuse that I thought I was just angry at what was happening. Anger was a part of it. But a more careful check unveiled that I was really scared—scared because I had no control over the situation. It's difficult for many of us men to admit that we are scared. We abhor powerlessness. But to ignore its existence is to subject ourselves all the more to its influence.

In assessing our emotions, we also are better able to measure our emotional resilience. I was aware, many times, that my resilience was running low. These were times of alert that I needed to increase my level of self-care and possibly seek additional professional care.

After assessing our thoughts and feelings, we gain a better idea of what we might need to do. As indicated in the previous paragraph, we might need to focus on self-care or find professional help. Some of the subsequent steps listed here also indicate possible actions to be taken.

## B. If Necessary, Contact the Appropriate Authorities

Until more recent years, my wife and I had separate counselors. There were times when I observed my wife slipping further into the darkness of despair. When I saw this happening, I went with her to her counseling. On some of those occasions, he readmitted her to the hospital.

In more urgent situations, you may need to call your local police or helpline. These are not easy steps to take, but they are necessary if suicidal thoughts intensify from ideation to intention.

## C. Determine What Responses Will Help to Stabilize the Situation.

I am not suggesting codependent acquiescence or enabling. I am recommending that we not fuel any fiery trauma with our own issues. This is why it is so important that we identify our own thoughts and feelings so that we don't further complicate the situation.

Remember that communication is not only *what* we say; it also includes *how* we speak, *why* we speak, and *when* we speak. Wisdom is found in the instructions from scripture. "Everyone should be quick to listen, slow to speak and slow to become angry (James 1:19)."

I am also instructed by the words of Constance Nightingale.

> As sexual abuse is the most unloving thing that can happen to a child, then love is the key to our healing… the love that is acceptance of the people we are. It's someone listening and believing, someone caring, and understanding the complex mix of our emotions; someone accepting all the rage, grief and terror we have concealed for so long; someone helping us to replace the old tape that told us we weren't worth anything, were guilty and dirty, with a true new tape that speaks of our value, our innocence and essential goodness, and of our ability to take control over our own lives, and to trust ourselves and others.[44]

## D. Pray Throughout This Process.

It is interesting to me as I read the New Testament that when the disciples did cry out to Jesus, their cry was right to the point. Their prayers were void of platitudes and often revealed less than positive attitudes. For example, during the storm at sea when Jesus appeared oblivious because He was asleep, their prayerful comment was, "Lord, don't you care that we are about to drown?"

I'm not suggesting that we hurl insults at Jesus. But I am noting that, in trauma, we are not going to formulate a formalized prayer that will someday be quoted, as is that of St. Francis of Assisi. Generally, "God, I'm desperately in need of your help!" will suffice. God hears the prayer of those who come to him in humility and dependence (Hebrews 4:14–16).

## E. Debrief With Your Counselor Subsequent to the Event and Take Steps For Self-Care.

## CONCLUSION

I know I loved and do love my wife. And I know you do too—otherwise, you would not bother reading this book. Nevertheless, I know that I'm not alone in how I tended toward making life about me for too many years. That's not to say that I've been totally cured of that self-centered approach to life. At least now I can more readily recognize it and choose healthier and more loving responses.

I've learned that the better question—rather than "Why can't she get over it?"—is "What can I learn from this?" As stated in the Introduction of this book, nothing has taught me more about God—His love and His presence—and more about myself than this journey toward individual and marital health.

I've allowed you a good look into my own life in this chapter. My *modus operandi* in my marriage was too often to think in terms of "How am I being affected?" I never liked being inconvenienced—and I still don't like it. But I've come to the point of realizing how self-centered such a response really is and how diminishing it is to my wife and the war she has fought against the abuse's effects.

I've learned a lot about her and my admiration for her has grown as I've recognized that the "it" in the question of this chapter is "trauma". I would never ask a war veteran when he or she will get over their trauma. It's unthinkable! So it is with our wives.

# Chapter Six: Personal Application

1. Multiple motives were noted as to why husbands ask "Why can't she just get over it." There can be a **selfless** motive of a man sincerely wishing that his wife could be freed of the pain. There can also be a **selfish** motive of a man no longer wanting his life and comfort to be interrupted with the pain. Identify your motive in asking the question and substantiate your answer.

2. Look over the diagnostic criterion for post–traumatic stress disorder in the DSM–5 in Appendix A. Record your observations of your wife's life experience next to the criteria that apply. The purpose of this exercise is not to diagnose your wife. Rather, the purpose is to use this exercise as a means of putting yourself in your wife's shoes.

3. When have you been aware of your own trauma as a secondary survivor? How did reading this chapter make you aware that you too have experienced trauma? Remember that recognizing our own trauma, as husbands and secondary survivors, is not for the purpose of casting us into fear and emotional paralysis. Rather, our recognition of our own sense of trauma prevents us from living in denial so that we can manage ourselves.

4. Read through Constance Nightingale's statement again. What do you learn from her statement and how can it shape your future responses to trauma?

For a more in-depth review of this chapter, we have also provided a full, free downloadable "Guide for Application" on our website:
www.marriagereconstructionministries.org.
It is our hope that the additional questions in this guide will take you further into potential personal and marital growth.

Chapter Seven

# WHAT DO I DO WITH MY ANGER TOWARDS HER PERPETRATOR?

Years had passed since I first learned of the sexual abuse inflicted upon my wife as a young child. All that time, I'd felt hatred toward the man who had cut such a deep and jagged wound into my wife's soul. How could I possibly be at peace with his perversion? He was the dark villain in an ongoing horror movie.

But then we learned where he lived. We met people who knew him. He was within reach. It was now in the realm of possibility to confront this vile creature. Knowing his location created a tangible figure in my mind that unleashed a rage I had never known before. I was aware of my vague hatred, but never was murder on that list. Suddenly, it was.

As a pastor for over twenty–five years, I'd studied enough, preached enough, and lived enough to know about the destructive force of rage. But rage that had lain dormant for so many years was now flooding my mind and soul, creating a force I wasn't sure I could resist.

The distance from our home to his would involve hours, even days of travel, but that wouldn't matter. The trip would offer all the more time to salivate over his impending doom. I pictured him writhing in pain and pleading for mercy. Why would I extend mercy?

This man had violated my wife's personhood and sexuality. My daughters and I experienced daily trauma as we witnessed her battle to live. I stood by helplessly as I watched my wife be admitted to a four–week stay in a psychiatric ward. I awakened almost nightly to her cries and calls for help as she continued to experience nightmares. Fears overwhelmed me as I witnessed irregular eating habits and her suicidal ideation.

I wanted to tie the guy down and cut him apart, piece by piece. Slowly. Her pain lasted for over forty–five years, I wanted his to last at least forty–five minutes. The prospect of my inevitable arrest and incarceration did nothing to appease my craving for inflicting pain upon this monster and invoking what I believed to be justice. My fantasy was ruthless and my rage relentless. It did strange things to my soul. I could not quiet the storm. I was drowning in deep waves from which I could find no rescue. My prayers echoed in empty space.

To be enraged was rational. C. E. Barshinger stated in *Haunted Marriage*, "Sexual abuse of children is akin to psychic murder."[45] Injustice is inflicted upon an innocent, helpless, trusting child, an injustice that inflicts a deep injury and permanent wound.

My rage, however, was not limited to the injustice done to my wife. I was enraged because I felt violated. I had been robbed too. Robbed of intimacy. Robbed of normalcy. But living with rage is not a good arrangement.

I knew better than to explode at people, but my rage often seeped through when I sought to dominate and maintain control both at home and at work. My occasional visits to a counselor brought relief but not resolution.

In the words of Frederick Buechner, I was "wolfing down myself." Buechner said,

> Of the Seven Deadly Sins, anger is possibly the most fun. To lick your wounds, to smack your lips over grievances long past, to roll over your tongue the prospect of bitter confrontations still to come, to savor to the last toothsome morsel both the pain you are given and the pain you are giving back—in many ways it is a feast fit for a king. The chief drawback is that what you are wolfing down is yourself. The skeleton at the feast is you.[46]

Trapped in my self–consuming rage, I began calling out to a few trusted friends, hoping that somehow my cries of despair and their prayers would reach the ears of God. I became vulnerable before my staff members by laying aside my perceived power, letting them see through the window of my soul, and allowing them to pray over me.

One of the most challenging things for a husband whose wife is the survivor of childhood sexual abuse is to forgive his wife's perpetrator(s). I have asked numerous husbands of survivors of childhood sexual abuse about their journey in forgiving their wife's perpetrator. Quincy's response was, "I'd certainly want him brought to some kind of justice." Clay said that he didn't even respect the memory of his wife's perpetrator. He wondered, "Am I supposed to forgive this guy for what he did to my wife when she was a young girl? I'm still struggling with that point." Nigel, on the other hand, said, "You've got to forgive because of biblical instruction." No one can be a member of humanity without colliding with some insult or offense that invites forgiveness as a response. The severity of the cruelty may vary, but the certainty of some infraction is common to all of us. I sit here and think of...

- People whose family members have been mercilessly beheaded by ISIS terrorists
- High school students and younger who are bullied by false claims splattered across the screens of social media
- Husbands and wives whose entire savings have been gambled away without their knowledge by their gambling–addicted spouse
- Business owners betrayed by an employee's embezzlement
- Homeowners whose life possessions disintegrated in the blazing fire torched by a random arsonist
- Family members and neighbors whose elderly loved one was viciously murdered by an invading thief in the middle of the night
- A family member or friend who was killed in an auto accident caused by a drunken driver

None of these incidents are isolated. All of us have either lived in the tragedy or heard it reported in the news.

The theme of forgiveness is found in the ancient literature of Christianity, Buddhism, Islam, Hinduism, and more. Furthermore, the need for, and benefits, of forgiveness have been the pursuit of social research for the past three decades.

Among the most notable researchers has been Dr. Robert Enright, Professor of Educational Psychology at the University of Wisconsin— Madison and Co–founder of the International Forgiveness Institute. Enright and those who followed him have collectively documented how the practice of forgiveness fosters social well–being and grants multiple personal psychological and physiological benefits. While those of spiritual faith might only view forgiveness as an obligation, social research confirms that forgiveness is a pathway to healing for those who have been abused.[47]

Enright's work, *Forgiveness is a Choice: A Step-by-Step Process for Resolving Anger and Restoring Hope,* and other similar works written subsequent to the research offer some version of a pathway to forgiveness.[48] These pathways typically begin with an acknowledgement of the injustice done and recognition of its damaging effects. The pathways move from introspection to decision, a choice to forgive.

My struggle was not with *what* I needed to do in order to forgive but *how* to do it. In other words, the pathway might show me the movement, but where can I find the motivation? I seemed locked in my rage. I knew I was being devoured by my own rage. If I could have found something within myself to progress toward forgiveness, I would have jumped on the pathway years ago.

Am I describing your experience right now? Are you stuck in your rage? Do you have knowledge of forgiveness and its benefits but an apparent lack of motivation? Do you agree that forgiveness would be the best thing to do but find it almost impossible to free the perpetrator so that you can be free from hurt?

The next section invites you to explore a new perspective. In sharing my personal expedition, my intent is not to force my spiritual belief on you. But it is my desire to convey to you a discovery that has granted me the outcomes that are documented in the biblical record and supported by current social research.

### EXPLORING A NEW PERSPECTIVE

Let's go back to Nigel for a moment. Nigel said, "You've got to forgive because of biblical instruction." I know that seems like a rigid statement, but let's explore the ancient writing.

According to the biblical instruction, we are to forgive "just as in Christ God forgave" us (Ephesians 4:32). That explanation of how we are to forgive certainly does not make it any easier to forgive. But let's consider it before we dismiss it.

Within a few months of my request for intercession from my trusted friends, I sat in a communion service, not expecting much from the devotional being delivered by a pastor colleague of mine, symptomatic of an increasingly cynical heart that seems to accompany unchecked rage. Listening with indifference, I heard the word "forgiveness." I thought, *I've preached plenty of sermons on forgiveness. Is this brief devotional really going to offer me anything new?*

Moving quickly through his simple outline, he came to his second point: "Forgiveness means being willing to take the hit for the wrong done by someone else." The words came as a sledgehammer against my fortified wall of cynicism.

"Jesus took the hit for us when he hung on the cross." The words of my colleague echoed in my mind. "Forgiveness means being willing to take the hit for the wrong done by someone else."

At that point, a whisper in my soul began overriding my colleague's voice. I knew it wasn't me whispering to myself because I would not have been whispering what I heard within. I knew it was a God whisper: "Will you forgive your wife's perpetrator by taking the hit?" As though that was not personal enough, God got even more personal: "Will you end the self-pity when her wounds affect you? I took the hit for you on the cross. Will you identify with me in a fuller dimension by taking the hit as a small reminder of what it cost me to take the hit for the perpetrator and for you?"

By the way, as a side note here, if you are thinking that you are a relatively good person, I'll take you at your word for now. But I know two things about myself. First, I cannot even keep my own rules, not to mention keeping God's rules (i.e., commandments). Second, there's no way in the world that I'd want the full record of my thoughts and actions to be put on video for all to see. I know what I've done. I know what I've thought… and so does God.

As I sat in that communion service, I was just like the people in the biblical record. I was like Jacob as a man left alone and wrestling with God (Genesis 32:22–32). I was Isaiah saying, "Woe is me" as I knew the heavy hit that my own sin inflicted upon the Son of God (Isaiah 6:5). I became like Peter as Jesus queried into his soul and now mine, several times, "Do you love me? (John 21:15–17)."

The communion service was nearing its conclusion. I sat in the cushioned chair with my muscles aching as I attempted to control my visible shaking. Tears could not be held back. I worked to calm my choking from such a tightly knotted throat.

It seems scandalous and ludicrous to forgive a sexual perpetrator. How can the husband of a childhood sexual abuse survivor possibly follow the biblical command to "Get rid of all bitterness, rage and anger, brawling and slander, along with every form of malice. Be kind and compassionate to one another, forgiving each other, just as in Christ God forgave you (Ephesians 4:31–32, NIV)?"

If forgiveness is going to be genuine, it is essential that we grasp what forgiveness is and what it is not. Here are six key points about forgiveness.

### 1. Forgiveness in Relationships is Based on Covenant, Not Contract.

Dr. Greg Boyd has noted that unless we forgive as God, in Christ, has forgiven us, we are inclined toward quid pro quo forgiveness. Quid pro quo forgiveness is getting something for something: a favor for a favor. Quid pro quo is when my forgiveness is conditional on someone being brought to justice or paying some kind of retribution. It is contractual. God does not seek a contractual quid pro quo relationship with us.

God offers us a covenantal relationship rather than a contractual arrangement. Scripture depicts covenantal life as receiving God's life and then expressing it: "Freely you have received, freely give (Matthew 10:8)." Forgiveness, therefore, is about receiving God's forgiveness and then expressing it to others:

*For if you forgive other people when they sin against you, your heavenly Father will also forgive you. But if you do not forgive others their sins, your Father will not forgive your sins. —Matthew 6:14–15*

As we express forgiveness, we grow more in our understanding of what it was for God to forgive, which then opens our hearts to increased gratitude and receptivity of His redemptive forgiveness. It is a cyclical flow, as Boyd notes.[49]

### The Cyclical Flow of Forgiveness

GOD

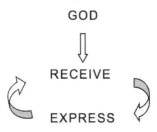

RECEIVE

EXPRESS

God extends His perfect forgiveness to us, and we receive it freely. As we genuinely receive forgiveness, we express forgiveness. The more we receive it, the more we can express it. The more we express it, the more we receive it.

Genuine forgiveness is grounded in the forgiving work of God through Jesus Christ. Without His work, we are more inclined towards a quid pro quo form of forgiveness.

## 2. Forgiveness Is Not Without Cost.

Forgiveness was not without cost to God the Father. "For God so loved the world that he gave his one and only Son, that whoever believes in him shall not perish but have eternal life (John 3:16)."

Forgiveness was not without cost to God the Son,

> *Who, being in very nature God, did not consider equality with God*
> *something to be used to his own advantage;*
> *rather, he made himself nothing by taking the very nature of a servant,*
> *being made in human likeness. And being found in appearance as a man,*
> *he humbled himself by becoming obedient to death—*
> *even death on a cross! —Philippians 2:6–8*

Forgiving "just as in Christ God forgave us" means that we take the hit for the offense just as Christ did for us (Ephesians 4:32 NIV). In other words, forgiveness includes accepting the cost of the effects of childhood sexual abuse without holding it against the perpetrator.

## 3. Forgiveness Does Not Nullify Legal Consequences.

Forgiveness of the perpetrator does not nullify consequences established by law. It is not the same as granting a pardon for the offense. Outgoing governors and presidents often pardon selected criminals. But their pardon does not mean forgiveness. Neither does forgiveness mean pardon from the consequences.

## 4. We Don't "Forgive and Forget."

Forgiveness does not mean forgetting. The true graciousness of forgiveness can only be exercised when we are fully aware of what occurred, and we still choose to forgive.

## 5. Forgiveness Is Not Acting As Though No Wrong Was Done.

Forgiveness does not mean that the action being forgiven is condoned or tolerated. When Jesus forgave the woman caught in adultery, he instructed her, "Go now and leave your life of sin (John 8:11)."

## 6. Forgiveness Is Not the Same As Reconciling.

Forgiveness does not require reconciliation. Forgiveness of the perpetrator does not even require an encounter with the perpetrator because it is a transaction within the soul of the husband and survivor.

Coming back to that communion service and my wrestling with God, I finally began spiritually stuttering through my prayer of response.

> *"Lord, my words seem so simple when the turmoil and rage are so overpowering. I'm not even sure I know how to surrender. How do I know with certainty that I am responding to you 100 percent? What do I do? Do I just say the words?... Lord, I surrender the rage. I let go of it. You take it. Trying to be as honest as I can be right now. I forgive the perpetrator. I agree to accept the hit."*

My words of surrender seemed awkward. But God heard, and He did what was incomprehensible to me. He transformed my intended action of rage and the infestation of rage in my heart.

The rage is gone. Once forgiveness was granted, I was no longer controlled by the anger, and the perpetrator was rendered powerless over my life.

My wife has gone through years of counseling and has experienced God's healing. She now mentors other women who are survivors of childhood sexual abuse and delights in sharing her story of God's faithfulness in and through trauma. She speaks at women's retreats and leads workshops on the topic of childhood sexual abuse and forgiveness. I am consistently amazed at how God has taken this horrible event in her life and used it as a catalyst for something great.

Do I still feel the pain? Yes, enough to remind me of my commitment to take the hit—but even more as a reminder of the hit taken for me. For good reason, there is still pain. But the raging winds of desire to act on that pain have been calmed. Prior to the day of that memorable communion devotional, the raging ocean of my soul frightened me. Since that day, I've been amazed by the extent of God's gracious gift of freedom.

## ESTABLISHING NEW PATTERNS

There are identifiable steps as we move towards being released from our rage. Each step requires sufficient time to honestly assess our attitudes, motives, and intentions. This is not a hurried process, and no two people will travel through these steps at the same pace. Progress is what matters.

Though there is some sequential movement through these steps, there is no solid line between them. At times, we will find it necessary to revisit earlier steps. In fact, we will occasionally discover the need to go back through the entire process and forgive at a deeper level. This is often the case when the effects of the abuse exert renewed trauma on our wives. But with each journey through the steps, the forgiveness becomes deeper, and we become freer.

### Step 1: Admit Your Anger and Rage and Accept Responsibility For Your Feelings.

My interviews with husbands of childhood sexual abuse survivors indicated how men have varied responses to anger. I observed three different categories for describing their anger: (a) indulgent, (b) indignant, or (c) unidentified.

> **a. Indulgent Anger:** My form of anger was indulgent. As I noted earlier in this chapter, I was the "poster child" for the self–consuming anger that Frederick Buechner warned would lead to "wolfing down myself." My indulgence in the tantalizing fantasy of revenge neither alleviated my anger nor initiated any form of justice. To the contrary, my indulgence extended the perpetrator's ravaging wound beyond my wife and allowed it to include my own soul. It exacerbated my own gloom and contaminated my soul.

> **b. Indignant Anger:** For some husbands, anger seethed in the form of indignation towards the perpetrator. Chad's wife, Barb, was abused by her father for four years. Depression and sexual preoccupation marked her adult life. Chad acknowledged his anger at her father in his statement: "I'm angry at this evil man. To this day, I don't have any respect. At his funeral, I couldn't speak. There wasn't anything that was going to get me to go and speak at his funeral." Whereas indulgent

anger wishes to physically exterminate the perpetrator from human existence, indignant anger is more a means of mentally exterminating the perpetrator from conscious existence.

**c. Unidentified Anger:** I discovered a negative correlation between a husband's anger and his practice of bottling-up his feelings. The more that husbands bottled-up their feelings, the less they perceived their anger. Nelson's wife of twenty-seven years had been sexually abused by her father during her teen years. The effects upon his wife and their marriage included her multiple affairs, emotional distancing from Nelson, and frequent bouts of anger. Nelson, with his unidentified, bottled-up anger, stated, "I'm not an angry person. I mean, I have a temper, don't get me wrong, but I'm not [angry]." Nelson did not perceive himself as angry unless his anger was visibly expressed.

Whether our anger is indulgent, indignant, or unidentified, it exists. Whether we entertain it, rename it, or disregard it, its damaging effect cannot be escaped. We are consumed by it unless we admit and accept responsibility for it.

In addition to our anger's affect upon us, it also has an injurious effect on our spouse as a survivor of childhood sexual abuse. Our unacknowledged anger can affect our moods, tone of speech, patience with our kids and others, sleep, emotional resilience, and many other aspects of our daily living. Our wives, as intuitive observers, will keenly sense our inner disturbance and will perceive that disturbance as being directed at her. And, if we husbands are truthful with ourselves, we must acknowledge that there are times when our anger is directed at our wives; even though it should be aimed at her perpetrator. A wife's detection of her husband's anger will distance her emotionally from her husband, thereby sabotaging the ability of both husband and wife to deal with the real issues together. Our connection as husband and wife is compromised unless we admit and accept responsibility for our anger.

**Step 2: Respond Appropriately Toward The Perpetrator.**

Our response may include legal action against the perpetrator. Taking such action is not incongruous with forgiveness. Remember, forgiveness does not nullify legal consequences and does not act as though no wrong was done.

Legal action can be pursued with honorable motives. Seeking justice is an example of an honorable motive since justice is about maintaining moral uprightness and decency. To dismiss justice, if it is a viable option, would be to diminish the offense and demean the offended, our spouse. To seek justice unveils the offense and advocates for the survivor.

Another honorable motive for seeking legal action is the effort to bring protection to any other victims or potential victims of the perpetrator. To remain silent is to allow the perpetrator to continue his/her atrocity against other innocent children.

Vengeful action, however, fails to alleviate anger or initiate justice. Granted, many victims of numerous crimes have pursued justice in the court system while lodging a murderous spirit within. Our goal, however, must be to seek for matters to be settled not only within the court system but also within the confines of our own soul.

## Step 3: Redirect Our Thought Patterns.

Our rage can sometimes be misdirected. This misdirection also occurs with the survivor. The survivor's rage toward her offending perpetrator is sometimes so explosive that its shrapnel hits and wounds those in close proximity, often her husband.

The rage within a husband can also be easily misdirected. When a survivor's anger is fired at her husband, many men opt to fire right back with anger. Or if a husband becomes frustrated with the effect that the childhood sexual abuse is having on his wife, his frustration may easily emit in anger towards his wife, especially if he thinks she should be able to "just get over it."

An initial step is for us, as husbands, to realize the true offender. Just as we are not to be confused with the perpetrator in our wives' minds, so also, they should not be in the line of fire for our anger. The effects of childhood sexual abuse that our wives bear were not self–inflicted. The offensive trauma endured by our wives as innocent children was brought about by intentional, intrusive, and insidious actions inflicted by a self–serving, conniving, and thoughtless perpetrator. Anger towards that perpetrator is a rational response.

But there is a further crucial step in the process if we are to progress toward forgiveness. Eventually, the rage we have held against the *offender* for what he or she has done needs to be redirected to rage at the *offense* for how it has wounded our wife.

God Himself hates the offense of the perpetrator. The Old Testament writer Solomon, known for his wisdom, spoke of God's intensified scorn towards those actions that are injurious, prejudicial, are divisive towards others.

> *Here are six things GOD hates,*
> *and one more that he loathes with a passion:*
> *eyes that are arrogant,*
> *a tongue that lies,*
> *hands that murder the innocent,*
> *a heart that hatches evil plots,*
> *feet that race down a wicked track,*
> *a mouth that lies under oath,*
> *a troublemaker in the family.*
> *(Proverbs 6:16–19, The Message)*

The redirection of our rage from our wives to the offender and from the offender to the offense is an intentional, sequential, and purposeful process. The goal is twofold: (a) to release any self–centered anger—anger that is focused on how we are affected, and (b) to grow in our value of justice and our care for others, loathing any actions, including our own, that are detrimental to others.

The redirection of rage has multiple potential, beneficial outcomes. First, our redirected anger that concentrates on the offense can increase our empathy for our wives as survivors who endured the offense. Second, redirecting our anger can ultimately free us from the control that the perpetrator held over us when we remained in our rage. Third, anger that is redirected to the offense can potentially lead us to constructive actions that will uphold justice.

> *Hate evil, love good;*
> *maintain justice in the courts.*
> *(Amos 5:15, NIV)*

**Step 4: Progress Toward Forgiveness.**

You may be wondering why so much time and content has been devoted to our anger and rage. Here's why:

> ➤ If we are dismissive of our anger, we will then be trivializing the gravity of the offense.
>> ➤ If we trivialize the offense, we then vindicate the offender.
>>> ➤ If we vindicate the offender, we will be indifferent to the trauma inflicted on the survivor, our wife, and thereby dismissive towards her personally.

This sequential digression egregiously repeats the tragic absence of care and protection from the adults who were supposed to be ensuring the protection of the survivor when she was a child. Sadly, a husband's dismissive response repeats the horror of her unheeded cry.

Furthermore, when the offensive and invasive violation of the offender is dismissed, any attempt at forgiveness will only be superficial. Without abhorrence of the offense, there cannot be genuine forgiveness of the offender.

The snag is that once we've been gripped by the gravity of the offense and have witnessed its wounding effect upon our wives, we discover that forgiveness is not our natural response. We find it easier—and even tell ourselves it is more satisfying—to resist extending grace to those who have sorely injured ourselves or those closest to us.

As I've conveyed earlier, my motivation to forgive came from outside of myself and not from within. God extended forgiveness and reconciliation to me through Christ. "For God was in Christ, reconciling the world to himself, no longer counting people's sins against them (2 Corinthians 5:19, NLT)."

*God makes it possible for us to extend grace to others because of the grace He has extended to us.*

# Chapter Seven: Personal Application

1. To what extent are you aware of your own anger or rage?

2. How is your anger/rage being expressed?

3. How are you being consumed by your anger or rage?

4. How can you adopt a new perspective in respect to the six points in the section Exploring a New Perspective?

5. Review the three responses to anger: indulgent, indignant, and unidentified.

    a. Identify your response to anger.

    b. What do you learn about yourself from your answer?

6. Begin progressing through the four identifiable steps towards forgiveness and being released from your anger and rage.

For a more in-depth review of this chapter, we have also provided a full, free downloadable "Guide for Application" on our website:
www.marriagereconstructionministries.org.
It is our hope that the additional questions in this guide will take you further into potential personal and marital growth.

Chapter Eight

# OUR SEXUAL RELATIONSHIP IS IN TROUBLE. WHAT SHOULD I DO?

Frustration is common in the sexual relationship for a husband whose wife has been sexually abused as a child. The effects of sexual abuse can be exhibited by compulsive sexual behaviors as well as the avoidance of sexual intimacy.

There are at least three reactions for husbands whose marital sexual relationship is affected by his wife's childhood sexual abuse: shame, emasculation, and trauma. Husbands of survivors experience any or all of those three reactions whether their wives avoid sexual intimacy or pursue sexual promiscuity.

## 1. Shame

Shame can be activated through our relationships when the connection between two people is disrupted. I don't have any memories of my dad raising his voice at me when I was growing up. But he had a certain look of disapproval that activated shame in me every time. It did not have to be in an actual wrongdoing; it was typically just not measuring up to an expectation. When I got the look, I didn't talk back. Instead, I just looked away or looked down, disconnected from the one I wanted to please.

Shame occurs in the relationships that matter to us, like those with our wives. When that relationship is disrupted for some reason, there is an automatic emotional reaction within us that is shame.

The disconnection can certainly occur through harsh or thoughtless words. But words are not even necessary. A look can activate shame. And certainly, an action—or a failure to act—from a loved one can activate shame.

Jyl was only three years old when her father began entering her bedroom at night and sexually abusing her. His frequent perpetration continued for ten years. As a result, Jyl experiences a strong aversion to sexual expression in adulthood.

Wes, Jyl's husband, acknowledged his struggle due to Jyl's lack of sexual desire. He stated, "When you realize that your wife isn't enjoying that part of your life, it makes you feel like you're being very selfish." The disconnect Wes had with his wife imposed upon him the shameful and mistaken sense that something was wrong with him.

Chad's wife was entangled in habitual sexual stimulation and experimentation. There were times when he would walk into their bedroom when she was engaged in her ritual. The words Chad used to describe what he saw were *bizarre, insatiable, unbelievable,* and *vile.* He stated, "I couldn't cope with it." Chad was shut out from connection with his wife because of her self-indulgent sexual preoccupations. Their disconnect resulted in shame. Chad's shame was not because he was excluded from her lust, but because was excluded from her love.

## 2. Emasculation

Modern-day definitions and usage of *emasculation* include the idea of *being deprived of* vigor, strength, and sense of manhood. In other words, emasculation can occur emotionally as well as physically. Emotional emasculation can be inflicted verbally. *AskMen* reported the statements women might make—many times aimed at making us better men—that result in the deprivation of vigor in the man, especially when made publicly rather than behind closed doors.

- You desperately need a haircut.
- There is no way you're still a medium.
- Didn't I just buy you deodorant?

And the deadliest of all—

- I faked it.[60]

For husbands of women who are survivors of childhood sexual abuse, emasculation can occur sexually. The infrequence or absence of sexual intimacy communicates to a husband that he should just keep his sexual organs hidden, out of sight and away from touch. Though he doesn't have to experience the pain of physical castration, he endures the pain of emotional and sexual emasculation.

For several days, Nathan, a husband of a survivor, tried to keep his frustration over the lack of sexual intimacy to himself. After noticing his demeanor, Nathan's wife asked, "What's wrong?" His response was, "Testosterone. That's what's wrong. I have it! I wish I didn't!" Nathan's response, though peppered with sarcasm and frustration, manifested his sense of emasculation. Nathan was deprived of any expression of his appropriate desire for sexual intimacy with his wife, a deprivation that even led, at times, to a dislike of his own sexual drive and desire. At some level, husbands might even sense that sex must be bad or that they are bad if it is such a struggle.

Roger, another husband of a survivor, referred to feeling "cheated" of sexual intimacy. He also spoke of the emptiness and loneliness because "there was nobody that understood."

Emasculation also occurs when the survivor is engaged in sexual promiscuity or, as in Chad's case, is engaged in self–stimulation and experimentation. As Chad said, "I couldn't cope with it." Chad was shut out from connection with his wife because of her self–indulgent sexual preoccupations. Her actions nonverbally communicated to Chad that he was not enough, leaving him deprived of his sexual expression.

### 3. Trauma

Counselors and researchers of human behavior have observed that trauma can be transmitted from the traumatized person to others with whom the victim is in close relationship (e.g., abuse survivor to husband). People surrounding the traumatized victim can experience what is known as secondary trauma, and they are called secondary survivors.

Secondary trauma commonly occurs in the context of the sexual relationship. Both the survivor's phobic reaction to sexual intimacy or her compulsive preoccupation with sexual activity—the effects of childhood sexual abuse can lead to either extreme—impose trauma upon her husband. Survivors often subconsciously confuse the present intimacy of love and trust with the past injury of violation and hurt. The survivor's flashbacks and related stress can then transmit trauma to the partner.[51]

In some cases, the pure and appropriate sexual intimacy of a married couple in their bedroom can become a reenactment of the traumatic sexual abuse endured by the survivor. The husband of the survivor is unsuspecting and sometimes unaware of this "rerun" that is occurring in his wife's mind and emotions.

During their dating years, Dan & Nikki abstained from sexual intimacy so that their experience on their wedding night could be filled with newness and mutual devotion. They looked forward to their wedding night intimacy with great and glad anticipation.

Dan described what happened when they got to their hotel room.

> *Like every groom, I'm like, "Goody." And, literally began to unzip the top of her wedding dress and she just broke down in tears. Just broke down in tears... when that [the tears] happened,... it was like, "All right, game on. What's happened here?"*

Five or six years into the marriage, Dan noted that the problem of Nikki's avoidance of or phobic reactions to sexual intimacy "became more acute." She'd pull the sheet and blankets up covering her entire face. Dan knew about Nikki's childhood sexual abuse going into their marriage. But he was not prepared for the disappointment, frustration, and trauma he experienced from Nikki's phobic reactions to sexual intimacy. He summarized this unsettling aspect of their relationship by saying, "Anytime we got around trust and physical intimacy like sexuality... wheels off."

Dan, as other husbands of child sexual abuse survivors are, was a secondary survivor experiencing secondary trauma. Husbands of survivors experience a trauma—that they would not have otherwise experienced—as a result of their wives' primary trauma as primary survivors.


## EXPLORING A NEW PERSPECTIVE

The complexity of human sexuality makes it challenging as we explore a new perspective that will help us navigate through the shame, emasculation, and trauma. Whether or not the perspective explored here is new for you, it will lead to renewed thinking in regard to our sexuality and intimacy.

## 1. Our Wives' Struggle With Sexual Intimacy Makes Total Sense

Abuse teaches a girl several twisted ideas about her body: that it is unsafe, dirty, and evil. As noted earlier, Nikki's thoughts about her body were filled with shame as she covered herself with the bed sheet, even covering her face. Knowing that another man had committed a sexual violation using her body, it made no sense to her that her husband would want to look upon her. Her behavior was not healthy, but it made sense to her.

Whereas Nikki concealed her body in shame, the response of some survivors to childhood sexual abuse is to idolize their body in an insatiable pursuit of physical pleasure. Since the perpetrator used her body for his illicit pleasure, she reasons that there must be a sensuous pleasure to be found through it for herself. As a result, she sacrifices meaningful relationship for the pleasure that her body might bring her. In truth, she will never be satisfied, but the pursuit makes sense to her.

Our bodies are designed to be responsive to touch. Sexual touch can bring pleasure and arousal; that's how we were made. Even though the touch experienced in sexual abuse is a violation of a young girl's body, it can still cause arousal. This brings confusion to the young girl being abused. How can something that seems so wrong still bring a good physical feeling?

Consequently, in the girl's mind, her body betrayed her and is to be punished or sold. The survivor holds her body responsible for the wrong done to it and can blame her body for its appeal. Self-injurious behavior can be one means of punishing her body. A survivor might resort to the ritual of cutting. Survivors might also punish their body by selling it as a commodity. Women in prostitution and pornography use their body as an instrument of power. But her pursuit of power further punishes her body by reducing it to a sales product of "goods and services."

Whether or not a survivor is conscious of the motivation driving her behavior, the behavior can be explained. Her thinking is not healthy, and her conclusions are not true, yet there is a rational explanation for her behaviors. It all makes sense to her.

Husbands can benefit from having knowledge of the survivor's thinking. This knowledge is not to serve the husband so that he can "get his wife straightened out in her thinking," but so that he can appreciate all that she is up against in her thinking. Imagine how potent her pain is to overcome. Realize it is this pain that informs her behaviors and thwarts her capability to experience sexual intimacy as a wonderful experience that has been designed by God.

## 2. There Is Significance To Be Found Outside The Bedroom.

There is more than one way of describing wholeness—what it means to be a whole person and have a sense of wholeness. For me, my growing sense of wholeness is met through three concepts: identity, intimacy, and empathy.

### a. Identity

There's an inquiry that I sometimes ask people when I am first getting to know them. I'll ask it of you. I wish I could ask it over a cup of coffee with you at some café but this will have to suffice:

*Tell me something about yourself that you'd like me to know.*

The hesitancy some people have as they figure out how to respond is sometimes more revealing than their actual answer. For some, it appears difficult to self–reveal. It appears in some situations that people are asking themselves, "How do I want to be identified?" So how do you define or describe your identity?

Most men find their identity in what they do. Their occupation often serves as the foundation of their identity. "I'm a lawyer," "I'm a sales representative," or "I'm a laborer." Men in retirement years can become depressed if their occupation was their basis of identity.

Similarly, men can choose to find their identity in their accomplishments. I remember walking into a gentlemen's office and being amazed at his choice of décor. The walls did not contain pictures of his family or photography of scenery. Instead, all four walls were covered with plaques and certificates of awards. No doubt, this man did some wonderful things and was probably duly recognized. But I got the distinct impression that even all the awards were not enough because of his effort to make sure that those around him knew what he had done.

Other men have opted for a more relational approach and have found their identity in their role. A primary example of this form of identity is the man who proudly declares, "I am the father of three children," or "My children are my #1 priority." This seems admirable in that their energy is focused on a longer-term investment. However, they too can become disoriented and depressed when their children choose a different path or lifestyle than what the father had intended. I've watched such men question everything about themselves as dads.

Men can also choose to find their identity in their physicality, masculinity, and sexuality. These men can be single, married, or married acting like they are single. Their physical appearance and sexual experience is their recipe for happiness. However, as they live to fulfill their physical and sexual desire, their emotional emptiness and hunger gnaws away deep within.

Having outlined some of the foundations of identity that we choose, I think through my own pursuit and experience. If someone asked me who I was, there would have been many times and years that my answer would have been grounded in one of the foundations I've identified. How about you? Who are you? How do you answer?

Foundations of identity that are attached to this temporal world can only offer temporary satisfaction and stability. Since we are created in the image of God (Genesis 1:27), we are designed not only as physical beings but also as spiritual beings—possessing a soul that is eternal. Therefore, the foundation of our identity must be rooted beyond the physical, or temporary, in the spiritual, or lasting.

We are healthiest when our identity is grounded not in what we do but in who we are. So who am I? I've learned—yes, I had to learn it—that I am loved by God. And being loved by God is like no other love experienced on this earth. It is unconditional. It is eternal. It is incomprehensible. Here's how the certainty of this love is described in scripture:

> *For I am convinced that neither death nor life,*
> *neither angels nor demons, neither the present nor the future,*
> *nor any powers, neither height nor depth,*
> *nor anything else in all creation, will be able to separate us*
> *from the love of God that is in Christ Jesus our Lord.*
> *(Romans 8:38–39, NIV)*

I know, right now you are thinking of some dark, hidden stuff in your life that you feel has put you on bad terms with God. Unfortunately, God is too often likened to a Heavenly Santa Claus whose actions and attitudes towards us are based on whether we've been naughty or nice. Not so!

I like what Brennan Manning has said: "Only to your lover do you expose your worst. To an amazed world Jesus presents a God who calls for [our] confession only so that he may reveal himself in a person's depths as his lover."[52]

Let me draw an analogy. Just as our wives' ability to disclose their childhood sexual abuse depends on their sense of safety, so also our ability to disclose our darkest secrets to God depends on our awareness that He loves us. Accordingly, a husband's love is his wife's safety.

This may not be what you were expecting to read in a chapter that deals with sex and sexuality. But if your marital struggles have included any form of disappointment, frustration, and feelings of rejection because your sexual intimacy has been thwarted, then the matter of our identity being grounded in God's love is of absolute importance. The more my awareness of how extraordinarily I am loved by God grows, the more I then find comfort, gain confidence, and experience acceptance in ways that cannot be offered by anything temporal.

### b. Intimacy

God created us distinct from all other living creatures. "God created mankind in his own image, in the image of God he created them; male and female he created them (Genesis 1:27)." In addition to our being made as physical and spiritual beings, God instilled in us some of the same capacities of His own: the capacity to feel, the capacity for social interaction and connection, the capacity to make decisions, etc.

As image bearers of God, "Adam and his wife were both naked, and they felt no shame (Genesis 2:25)." In other words, they had nothing hidden—no secrets. Everything they felt, every way in which they interacted and connected, all of their motivations were just as God intended for them. They were unhindered in fully knowing and being fully known (emotionally, mentally, spiritually, and sexually). Nothing was hidden.

Sex was AS IT OUGHT TO BE. Sexual desire was not a problem. Desire was perfect, just as God had designed.

Then, everything took a nosedive—theologically it's referred to as the Fall—when Adam and Eve decided with their God–given decision-making capability to do things their way, directly contrary to what God had instructed. From that day forward, sexuality and sexual intimacy has been wrought with problems.

But that was not the end of the story. Remember that God unconditionally, eternally, and incomprehensibly loves us. God came to Adam and Eve in the Garden—when they had gone into hiding—so that He could know and be known by them

At creation, God instilled the capacity for intimacy in us: to know and be known. Sadly, we sometimes choose to remain hidden, fail to live according to our God-given design for *intimacy*, and substitute human-driven and unfulfilling distortions. Instead of *intimacy*, we chase after *intensity*.

## Instead of intimacy, we chase after intensity.

*Intimacy* occurs when we know another fully and when we are also fully known. *Intensity*, the distorted substitute, desires power, surprise, shock, and boundary crossing. *Intimacy* leads to satisfaction and fulfillment. *Intensity* only leads to the need for more intensity. The driving force for *intimacy* is love for the other. The driving force for *intensity* can be our own anger and insecurity.

We benefit by examining our attitudes, motivations, and actions to discern if there are ways we've remained hidden rather than fully engaging in God's design for connection and intimacy. If we are not mindful of our God-given design, we then substitute human-driven and unfulfilling distortions.

I know that, just like Adam and Eve, you wish you and your wife could both be naked, facing and embracing each other. But knowing and being fully known is multi-dimensional. How much of yourself are you revealing to her? What does she know about you?

> *What makes you sad?*
> *What makes you angry?*
> *What makes you scared?*
> *What makes you happy?*
> *What makes you excited?*
> *What makes you feel tender?*

This is not about dumping your frustration on her by saying, "I feel so sad when we're not having sex." Nor is it managing her by saying, "I feel happy when you show interest in me." It isn't about unloading your fears on her either. It's about opening the window of your soul and letting her in. What makes you sad, angry, or scared at work and how do you resolve it? What happens with your friends or children that makes you happy, excited, or tender?

Being known involves risk. When I am willingly vulnerable, sharing my thoughts, emotions, motivations, etc., others know me, resulting in connection—intimacy. Is risk involved? Yes. Only God will love us unconditionally. But satisfaction and fulfillment are only possible when I take the risk.

I realize that some survivors of childhood sexual abuse are paralyzed emotionally. Their ability to reciprocate with feeling is compromised. But there is something to be gained if we take the risk of being vulnerable. Survivors want to feel safe, and safety can only be experienced when our wives know that we are being honest, real, and willing to be known.

*And may you have the power to understand, as all God's people should,*
*how wide, how long, how high, and how deep his love is...*
*Then you will be made complete*
*with all the fullness of life and power that comes from God.*
*(Ephesians 3:18–19, NLT)*

### c. Empathy

Empathy is knowing what it is to be you while simultaneously knowing what it is to be me. If you are lopsided with a greater focus on what it is to be you, then you become narcissistic. If you have greater focus on knowing what it is to be your wife, you become enmeshed or codependent in the relationship. A consistent simultaneous balance is necessary for a healthy relationship.

I have known what it is to be out of balance in both dimensions of empathy. I know what it is to make myself the center of the universe. I have also lived in codependency. My wife told me one day, "You are smothering me." I was obtuse to how I was smothering rather than empathizing.

In codependency, it is as if you have no will of your own. She feels good for a day, so you feel good for a day. She feels down, you're down. It's really no different from a puppet on a string, and she is the one who is in control—whether she wants to be or not.

Codependents are often thought to be partners of substance abusers. However, husbands of survivors can easily slip into codependency or may have even married because of codependency.

Codependency is a very complex issue that sabotages the health of any relationship. You may want to learn more about codependency if the following describes you. This list is drawn from Melody Beattie in her classic work *Codependent No More: How to Stop Controlling Others and Start Caring for Yourself.*

a. My wife's moods seem to control how I feel.

b. I usually feel responsible for how my wife feels.

c. I do all I can to please my wife but never really feel that I've done enough.

d. I can identify multiple ways that I tend to my wife's needs, but I cannot as easily identify how I've tended to my own needs.

e. I sometimes say yes when I really mean no.

f. My whole life seems to revolve around my wife's needs.[53]

Review these questions each day for the next week and determine what your attitudes and actions indicate.

By the way, it's easy to confuse codependency with sacrificial love. That's what I did. I smothered my wife with care the way I thought she would want to be cared for. I made my life all about making her happy, and I told her so. Meanwhile, she was watching me dissolve into a nondescript being who thought he had no needs or feelings of his own. I was imposing myself on her. That's when she told me that I was smothering her.

Think about that for a moment. Put yourself in the shoes of a survivor—as I eventually did—and consider what it feels like for a survivor to be smothered. Have you figured it out?

When a survivor feels smothered by her husband, or anyone else, it is like being abused all over again. When her perpetrator was abusing her, she was essentially being smothered. In other words, she could not get out from under his imposed will. I was replicating the act emotionally. Now for a more positive example. I pursued my doctorate while working full time in my ministry position. We all have times we look back on and wonder how we survived. My doctoral study was one of those times for me. After a quick supper that was prepared by my wife, I'd go to another part of our home and hibernate in my studies until late into the night. She lived as a doctoral widow.

And yet, it was during this crazy time of full-time work and study that my wife told me she felt more loved by me than ever. I had no idea how she could make that claim until years later when I came to an understanding of empathy. My doctoral research focused on the effects of childhood sexual abuse and their impact on marriage. My interviews with other husbands helped me to understand the wounds and the wounded better. I was learning what it was to be in my wife's shoes, and in so doing, I was learning how she needed and wanted to be loved.

So how does all of this pertain to the ways in which the effects of your wife's abuse is wreaking havoc on your sexual intimacy? Here's my answer. My own angst and wishes for freer and more frequent expression is lessened when I realize what it is to be in her shoes. No, we cannot disregard our own needs; that would not be healthy. But we can be alleviated of resentment and any sense of rejection when we realize that—with few exceptions—our wives are not consciously subjecting us to torture and punishment. They have been traumatized in such a way that has left them compromised of freely experiencing sexual intimacy.

In my own experience, sexual intimacy with my wife has been affected by her abuse in various ways and in various stages of our journey. Initially, I held the viewpoint that the effects of the abuse and the problems they presented to our intimacy surfaced years after her disclosure when she was dealing at a deeper level in her therapy with the reality of the abuse. The inner disturbance—which is necessary to progress toward healing—was affecting our intimacy... I thought. The fuller truth is that I was only half right. The full truth is that there was never a time when we were not affected by her childhood sexual abuse and by the baggage that I brought into our marriage myself. Though there were times when we both could say we enjoyed sex—before and after the disclosure—our enjoyment was skewed by unresolved issues for both of us. My controlling nature and my propensity to approach our sexual relationship as more of a physical performance than an emotional connection resulted in perspectives and practices that were not healthy. But I was not aware of my own emotional deficiency at the time. I lacked awareness of what it was to be me.

Empathy enables us to enter into intimacy more fully. Empathy also enables us to navigate through the disappointments when intimacy is hindered because of past abuse.

## ESTABLISHING NEW PATTERNS

I suspect that this chapter will be the first chapter that many men turn to in this book. I also assume that this section of the chapter might be one that many men jump to with the thought, "Just give me the answer!" or "Just tell me what to do to ease my sexual frustration."

If my suspicion and assumption are correct, then I need to ask you to go back to the beginning of this chapter and begin reading there. I have discovered that navigating through sexual struggles first requires some attitude adjustment as opposed to concentrating on behavior modification. Absorbing the preceding content of this chapter will serve to alleviate the feelings of frustration, depression, rejection, and low self–esteem that can occur when sexual intimacy is absent or infrequent in a marriage relationship.

There are three aspects for establishing new patterns: (a) there is a warning to be observed, (b) there is something to consider, and (c) there are steps to take.

### 1. Warning: Resorting to Pornography Will Add to Your Turmoil.

The use of pornography may seem so reasonable. If your wife cannot offer the intimacy you long for and that you expect in marriage, then why not find some sexual satisfaction if it can be done without getting involved with anyone else?

Not only does it sound reasonable, pornography is easily accessible. No one needs to know. It's private. No feelings get hurt, and no diseases get transmitted.

Pornography is here to stay. It's accessible through every internet device that we own. Young children can access it, and they do access it. Men and women no longer feel they risk their reputation by being "found out" in the public arena. Men whose wives experience aversion to sexual intimacy are especially vulnerable to its enticement.

What must we realize about pornography so that we do not add turmoil to our lives?

### a. Pornography Is Impersonal

God's creative design places sexual intimacy within relational intimacy, specifically and solely within the relational intimacy of husband and wife so that it preserves the quality of permanency. The union of our bodies as husbands with our wives is one dimension of God's multidimensional design which includes the emotional and spiritual intertwining of our souls. Without the multidimensional expression and experience of this marital and relational intimacy, "sex mutates into an isolating, loveless compulsion."[54] Emptiness is always the outcome of this mutated experience. A man considering the use of pornography needs to ask himself, "What does this lead to?" The answer is *emptiness*, complicated by the eventual desire for more that becomes a downward, spiraling plunge into madness.

The use of pornography changes a man from a lover to a consumer. When a man uses pornography, he goes shopping and orders up the model and the performance he desires. It's like being on a car lot of used cars or shopping on Amazon; it has nothing to do with a person or with love. In contrast, the marriage relationship is about knowing and being known as two people: being knit together in understanding, care, compassion, and acceptance.

Love cannot be found in pornography. In contrast to love, loneliness is intensified when pornography is used.

### Loneliness is intensified when pornography is used.

I've had husbands tell me that they feel cheated because their wives withhold sex from them. They therefore feel that they've been given a pass to resort to pornography. Groves makes the argument that lack of sex is not the problem. Lust is the problem, and it is never satisfied. He supports his case by asking this question, "Have you ever known a man who was satisfied to look at just one pornographic image over and over?" Every man who has battled with lust knows the answer to that question. So Groves concludes,

> If the most beautiful and digitally enhanced supermodel cannot keep a man from continually searching out new stimulation, why would he ever expect that his flesh–and–blood wife with her physical and spiritual flaws could succeed?[55]

A man's desire to use pornography originates within his own heart, not his bedroom.

## b. Pornography Affects a Man Neurologically

I received a phone call the other day from a longtime friend whom I have not heard from for a while. Our conversation was filled with questions of care, words of encouragement, nuances of understanding that are unique to our relationship, and laughter. In the days following, I repeatedly mentioned to my wife how delighted I was to receive that call and connect with my friend once again. It can be safely assumed that some dopamine had been released in my system when the call occurred.

Dopamine is a chemical that is released in our brains during pleasurable situations, and it can serve as a stimulant for us to seek out more of the pleasure. It is reasonable to believe that Adam and Eve experienced the release of dopamine and its effects. God intended it for good. But their Garden of Eden experience also informs us that what God intends for good can be distorted into uses that lead to destruction. So it is with the use of pornography. Joe Carter highlighted the neurological and relational distortion and confusion that results from the use of pornography.

> Dopamine surges when a person is exposed to novel stimuli, particularly if it is sexual, or when a stimulus is more arousing than anticipated. Because erotic imagery triggers more dopamine than sex with a familiar partner, exposure to pornography leads to arousal addiction and teaches the brain to prefer the image and become less satisfied with real–life sexual partners.[56]

## c. Pornography Uses Women.

If you disagree with this statement as a man, ask yourself if you would ever want your daughter to be filmed in a pornographic video or spread across the page of a magazine. To even write the sentence and pose the question repulses me.

The producers of pornography use women for their financial profit. And the consumers of pornography use the same women as though they were a commodity without a soul.

If you are using pornography, then consider this: How am I any different from the perpetrator of my wife? The perpetrator of childhood sexual abuse and the user of pornography both engage in using a person as an object, the former as a casualty of his power, the latter as a commodity for his pleasure.

## 2. Something To Be Considered

Though most guys are likely to engage in the practice of masturbation—that's what the statistics indicate—not many are likely to initiate a conversation about masturbation. Well, I just did!

In a study of couples who were in a period of involuntary celibacy, 79% of the men masturbated as a coping mechanism.[57] If you are one of the 79%—odds are that you are—you have probably wondered whether it is appropriate to masturbate.

Perhaps your mom or dad told you, "God doesn't want you doing that!" The misinterpretation of the biblical account of Onan in Genesis 38 has led some to believe that God punishes those who masturbate. Read the story again and you'll see that the account has nothing to do with masturbation.

Those from the Roman Catholic tradition, following Augustine, have traditionally held the view that marriage and sexual intercourse are for the purpose of procreation. Consequently, masturbation is viewed as a practice at odds with God's purpose. Protestants, on the other hand, look beyond procreation alone and view marriage for its intimate union and companionship, conveyed in the concept of cleaving and becoming one flesh (Genesis 2:24).

### a. Permission and Prohibition

The Bible does not mention or even allude to masturbation, suggesting that we may view masturbation as permissible. However, there are at least two dangers that would prohibit masturbation: (a) uncontrolled imagination, and (b) compulsion.

Masturbation becomes a snare when it takes our God–given imagination and plunges it into a world of godless desire and lust. A husband who envisions any woman other than his wife when masturbating is outside of God's design (Matthew 5:28). The specific danger of pornography has already been established. If we allow our own minds to be lured into the deceptive and conditioning messages of pornography and our sexualized culture, we then become associated with the same perversion as the abusive perpetrator(s) of our loved one—that young girls and women exist as mere objects for our own use/abuse. The imaging of a woman projected on the screen of a man's imagination potentially reduces her from a person with a soul to an object for his pleasure.

The second danger is the tendency for masturbation to evolve into a compulsion or obsession. Compulsive masturbation sabotages a man's ability to develop relationship with his wife and thwarts his ability to bring satisfaction to his wife.

Related to compulsive masturbation is the use of masturbation as a means of self-soothing. A good question that men can ask themselves as a means of monitoring the motive that is driving the masturbation is, "How old do I feel when I do this?" If the answer is something like twelve or sixteen, then further personal introspection is warranted. Why would you revert back to childhood or youth? What would help you to develop more emotional maturity? If you are aware of self-soothing as a motive, what other options do you have that don't result in shame and disappointment?

### b. Yearning vs. Lusting

The *Journal of Psychology and Theology* published an article titled "Theologically-Informed Education about Masturbation: A Male Sexual Health Perspective." In all the men's groups that I've participated in, I've never heard the words *theological* and *masturbation* used in the same sentence. The two authors of the article, Kwee and Hoover, distinguished between lust and masturbation.

Lust is characterized by self-centeredness, entitlement, and coveting. As has already been noted, masturbation can be driven by lust. But masturbation can also be driven by a motivation and desire that is apart from lust. Kwee and Hoover described masturbation as "the sexual expression of a fuller yearning for connectedness, i.e., connectedness that is not primarily sexual... Although he may not experience fulfillment from masturbation, he is at least striving for a deeper level of connectedness to another human being."[58]

Keeping in mind the moral boundaries established in Scripture and the potential dangers of masturbation, I suggest that it is possible for masturbation to occur within marriage as a yearning for connectedness rather than from a motivation of lust. This suggestion is intended for the husband whose wife cannot engage in sexual intercourse for a length of time and when masturbation does not rob her of sexual intercourse or intimacy.

## c. Openness vs. Isolation

When it is determined that masturbation is permissible, two commitments should be fulfilled in one's responsibility to their spouse. First, it is best when masturbation occurs with the spouse's knowledge and permission. Motivations should be discussed. This dialogue: (a) prevents the destructive habit of a solitary act that can inhibit one's ability to build relationship, (b) protects from lust, and (c) prevents depersonalization. In some cases, this dialogue with a survivor of childhood sexual abuse is not possible for a time. The trauma for some survivors prevents them from being reality-based. For example, a survivor may be repulsed at the normal occurrence of a husband waking up in the morning with an erection. It may be that a husband will need to wait until the survivor's health reaches the stage when he can bring the conversation about masturbation into the relationship.

Secondly, when masturbation occurs, the individual must keep thoughts within boundaries of reality and must center on the husband's longing for his wife and her alone.

## 3. Steps to Take

In addition to the guidelines already outlined in this chapter (e.g., guarding our imagination), I recommend three additional steps that can enhance the quality of life for husbands of sexual abuse survivors. The first is to ensure your self-care, the second is to enrich your intimacy, and the third is to have a conversation with your wife.

## a. Ensure Your Self-Care

During my times of personal struggle, I recall multiple occasions when a friend, mentor, or counselor asked me, "What need or desire are you trying to fulfill?" Another way of asking the same question is, "What need or desire is going unfulfilled right now in your life?"

All of us have desires and needs. This chapter has focused on our need for sexual intimacy. Desires are God-given. Counselors Mark and Debbie Laaser identify seven desires shared by all of us: the desire (a) to be heard and understood, (b) to be affirmed, (c) to be blessed, (d) to be safe, (e) to be touched, (f) to be chosen, and (g) to be included.[59]

But while our desires are God–given, the account of Adam and Eve teaches us that even in a perfect environment where every need is met, we can still seek to fulfill our desires in ways that are outside of God's design. This is important for men whose desire for more physical intimacy with their wife is unmet. We can be deceived into rationalizing that our choice for physical intimacy outside of God's plan is justified because our need is unmet within marriage. That rationalization is a smoke screen that hides a deeper problem.

Self–care begins with identifying healthy ways that our desires can be fulfilled and then taking action accordingly. Here are a few suggestions that have been very helpful to me.

• Developing relationships with other guys can make a big difference. I'm talking about spending time with men who have depth of character and with whom you have some common interests. My favorite times have often been having breakfast with a friend before heading off to work. There are two kinds of people: drainers and replenishers. Drainers suck the life out of you. Replenishers bring refreshing. Spend time and develop a deeper relationship with the replenishers in your life.

• Figure out what you love to do and build it into your schedule. During some of my difficult years, I discovered how enjoyable motorcycling could be. So I took lessons and bought a motorcycle that I could afford. Motorcycling made a huge difference in my stress level and well–being for many years.

• Exercise. Some guys love to jog or engage in some form of exercise. For me, exercise is a necessity. Whether exercise is your fun thing to do or a duty, as it is for me, do it. The link between our physical health and our mental and emotional health is undeniable.

• Find a counselor who maintains convictions that honor marriage. It may not work to share your sexual frustrations with other guys because it can be difficult for them to understand a marriage impacted by abuse. But a good counselor can help you process your disappointments and temptations.

## b. Enrich Your Intimacy

Some husbands endure years without sexual intimacy. Their wives remain at a distance sexually and emotionally. There are no easy answers, especially when the survivor resists going to a counselor.

At the same time, I know of a husband who took his wife on simple dates. They'd go out for ice cream. As simple as it was, it brought a level of satisfaction for him and afforded safety for her. Will she someday agree to sexual intimacy? The answer to that question is beyond his control. The important matter in their relationship is for him to love his wife in a manner that seeks to know her at whatever level she is willing to be known.

Intimacy includes being known. For husbands, this means being vulnerable with our wives: sharing who we are, what we think, and how we feel without any attempt to manipulate a particular response from her. It is about being known without winning our way. It means telling our wives about our day: what happened that was funny and what happened that was alarming. It means entering a memo into our phone or writing it down on a scrap of paper so that we remember to tell our wife when we're having supper together.

It is very difficult when there is lack of sexual intimacy in marriage. But some of the angst can be diminished when there is the development of emotional intimacy—the ability to be glad or sad together, to be connected in knowing each other deeply.

Others who have written about the impact of childhood sexual abuse on marriage also highlight the importance of emotional intimacy. Levine says,

> Many people are still unaware that intimacy can be expressed in other ways [than primarily through sexual relationship]. Without exploring other approaches to sharing your love for each other, the degree of intimacy gets stigmatized according to how your sexual relationship is. Subsequently, survivor and partner are set up for disappointment and emotional distancing. To help increase the level of intimacy in your relationship, you need to rekindle the romance.[60]

Another dimension that can fill our deep desires is to enrich our intimacy with God. If this sounds strange to you as a reader, I ask you to hear me out. If we think of our brains as a system of wires, the spiritual and sexual wiring of our brains overlap, intersect, and intertwine. This neurological circuitry indicates a practical outcome in real-life experience.

It is possible to experience a spiritual vitality through a consistently close relationship with God that lessens the aching when sexual intimacy is lacking. This is not to perceive God as a sexual partner. Instead, it is to experience the spiritual embrace of a God who fully knows us and infinitely loves us. This vitally intimate connection with God is possible because He has made Himself one–hundred–percent vulnerable in being fully known to us through creation, through His communication in the Word (the Scriptures), and through His Son, Jesus Christ.

> **It is possible to experience a spiritual vitality through**
> **a consistently close relationship with God**
> **that lessens the aching when sexual intimacy is lacking.**

Intimacy with God is when we know Him more fully and when we willingly make ourselves fully known to Him, hiding nothing. Men whose wives are hindered by their aversion to sexual intimacy can find full acceptance, inner strength and satisfaction, and a confident identity in knowing that nothing can separate them from God's love. I know I am not alone in being convinced of this. Paul, an educated and influential man, wrote:

> *I'm absolutely convinced that nothing—nothing living or dead,*
> *angelic or demonic, today or tomorrow, high or low,*
> *thinkable or unthinkable—absolutely nothing*
> *can get between us and God's love because of the way*
> *that Jesus our Master has embraced us*
> *(Romans 8:38–39, The Message).*

### c. Have a Conversation

When there is lack of sexual intimacy, some husbands aggressively communicate their frustration to their wives, and others avoid the conversation out of fear. I am an avoider. But first, I'll offer a few words to those who are more inclined to attack the problem more aggressively than I.

I do not know of any situations in which a husband has experienced true intimacy by aggressively complaining or commanding. I know that some guys are inclined to "just say it the way it is." They may feel better, momentarily, by "getting it off their chest." But as a guy dumps out all his angst, his wife ends up at the bottom of the pile that he has dumped. His unloading has only heaped more shame on her. She then spirals into her greater sense of failure.

Avoiders, like me, fear that their wives will give them the emotional "stiff arm." Yes, that might happen. She may distance herself for a time as she "runs" for safety. But in cases where husbands have invested themselves in enriching the emotional intimacy, their wives will not remain distanced and will "return" for emotional connection.

Communicating our desire to our wives must be out of empathy and love, remembering what it is to be in their shoes while simultaneously knowing what it is to be in our shoes. Therefore, it is appropriate to share our desire to be "naked and not ashamed" together, but to do so with all tenderness and understanding. Statements like "Do you know what it is to be a guy?" won't work. A husband's accusations and demands reveal his own distorted perception of sexual intimacy.

Remember Dan and Nikki earlier in this chapter? Nikki pulled the bed sheet up over her face, refusing to be known. She also had a wall of distrust built, not venturing beyond that wall to know Dan. Dan kept his sexual struggles from Nikki in their earlier years. But as Nikki experienced some healing through her counseling and support group, Dan eventually realized that sharing his struggles could become an opportunity for Nikki's ongoing development. Dan risked being vulnerable and empathetically expressed his desires to Nikki. In so doing, it calmed the waves of resentment that had built up in him, and it also offered Nikki the opportunity to experience further healing. For Dan and Nikki, his vulnerability in making his need known was worth the risk.

Hopefully, the day will come when your wife has discerned that she can trust you and has also discovered who she truly is sexually as a woman by having received some qualified counseling. In the meantime, the steps outlined in this chapter are not designed to solve the problem of infrequent sexual experience in your marriage by "getting her into bed." Instead, these steps are intended to bring serenity to the frustrations and temptations that go on in a husband's head.

## CONCLUSION

Intimacy is knowing and being known, requiring the revealing of myself as well as the exploring of the other. The exploration and revelation are mutual and multi-dimensional as noted in the following diagram:

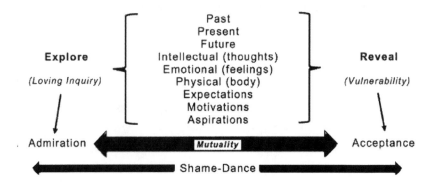

Intimacy deepens as three interactions increase.

**1. Mutuality:** Each individual is engaged in both exploring and revealing.
**2. Totality:** Exploration and revelation occur in all aspects of personhood and experience: past, present, future, intellect, etc.
**3. Vulnerability:** The exploration and revelation reach into deeper layers of the various aspects, requiring loving inquiry in the exploration and trusting vulnerability in the revelation.

Exploration is motivated by loving inquiry rather than probing interrogation. Its goal is to know rather than expose, to admire rather than assess, to esteem rather than blame. The purpose of the exploration is to discover.

Revelation is motivated by a willingness to trust; it is laying oneself bare, leaving nothing hidden. As with any expression of trust, revelation is accompanied by vulnerability and risk. Outcomes from the revelation are not known, and desired outcomes are not guaranteed. The purpose of the revelation is to uncover. Though outcomes are not guaranteed, the desired outcome of the discovery is increased admiration. The desired outcome of the uncovering is increased acceptance. Exploration as well as revelation are in the interest of the other.

As in any expedition, human exploration has some levels of inquiry that are more challenging than others. Some truths to be uncovered lie deeper or are more hidden than others. For example, segments of the past might be deeply buried in one's memory, or various motivations might be hidden from one's awareness. Consequently, the revelation is hidden from the person revealing as well as the person exploring. In the same way that earthquakes can bring buried ground to the surface, there are life events that can bring hidden aspects of personhood and experience to the surface of consciousness.

A key element in intimacy—knowing and being known—is to recognize the vast aspects of personhood and experience that are available for exploration and the immeasurable and mysterious depths that can be reached. It is crucial for husbands whose wives are averse to sexual intimacy to recognize the vast areas remaining to be explored. If sexual intimacy is lacking, there are many other areas to explore. The physical aspect might even warrant some exploration. While sexual intercourse might be "out of bounds" for your wife, perhaps other aspects of touch need to be explored. Some wives for whom intercourse is currently a seeming impossibility strongly desire other forms of touch: hand–holding or even kissing.

> **A key element in intimacy—knowing and being known—**
> **is to recognize the vast aspects of personhood**
> **and experience that are available for exploration and the**
> **immeasurable and mysterious depths that can be reached.**

The shame–dance is an unfortunate possibility when there is a disconnect in any aspect or dimension of the intimacy. The shame–dance can occur when your wife, a survivor of childhood sexual abuse, distances herself from you. The distancing might be emotional, physical, or both. It might be her refusal to share her thoughts (intellectual). While occasional distancing of one partner from the other is common in any relationship, the distancing in marriages with a survivor can be more distinct, distant, and disturbing.

This chapter has been written because your wife has distanced herself physically. There are several things to be remembered:

1. Explore what might still be physically safe for her and respond with acceptance.
2. Let your exploration be broadened. Her physical distancing does not rule out many other areas of who she is that can be and have yet to be explored.

3. Even when your wife might be in a dark place, keep the vision of the goodness of God's creation and His design in sexuality.

4. Move out of the shame–dance with a new step. Green and Pope offer four options for personal connection that can "diminish and release the shame:"

    a. Connect with a **Safe Other Person**.

        A safe connection is one that is with a person who is willing to be open (vulnerable) and is available, recognizing that no one is always available, and no one is always vulnerable.

    b. Connect with **Myself**.

        This is the recognition of:

            (i) what it is like to be me

            (ii) how I am feeling and

            (iii) what I am doing.

    c. Connect with the **Truth**.

        By asking ourselves "What is really happening?", we can challenge our assumptions and perceptions.

    d. Connect with **God**.

        Express to God what it is like to be me and explore what God has revealed about Himself.[61]

Think back to when you and your wife were dating. Everything was new. You probably talked for hours at a time. It was so romantic making those new discoveries of who she was and what she had experienced in life. Regardless of how long you've been married, there is more to be discovered, more ways to be drawn closer together.

Explore! Lovingly inquire. Allow your own inquisitiveness to be renewed and your love to be reignited. Accept her in all the potential aspects of intimacy.

# Chapter 8: Personal Application

1. In what ways have you experienced any of the three reactions shame, emasculation, and trauma of husbands to their wives' avoidance of sexual intimacy or pursuit of sexual promiscuity?

2. Empathy is knowing what it is to be you (i.e., your wife) while simultaneously knowing what it is like to be me (yourself).

    a. Describe your empathy with your wife.

    b. Are there aspects of you that are hidden? What are those aspects, and what would it take to make them known?

3. Has your sexual experience shown you to be a lover or more of a consumer? How so?

4. This chapter compared the consumers of pornography with perpetrators of childhood sexual abuse. What is your response to this comparison?

5. If you are aware of self–soothing as a motive, what other options do you have that don't result in shame and disappointment?

6. Go back to the diagram in the conclusion of this chapter. Once again, read through and think through the explanation accompanying the diagram.

    a. List four actions steps you will take, based on the diagram, to nurture the further development of intimacy with your wife.

For a more in-depth review of this chapter, we have also provided a full, free downloadable "Guide for Application" on our website: www.marriagereconstructionministries.org.
It is our hope that the additional questions in this guide will take you further into potential personal and marital growth.

Chapter Nine

# WHY IS IT SO DIFFICULT TO COMMUNICATE WITH MY WIFE?

Conflict occurs in all marriages, not just in the marriages of couples who are dealing with the effects of childhood sexual abuse. But conflict in marriages affected by childhood sexual abuse can be more frequent, unpredictable, and focused on issues not covered in the popular marriage books.

Many husbands of survivors that I talk to are frustrated over the social relationship with their wives. Some of Roger's conflict with Beth was due to her lack of assertiveness even if it meant disagreeing with him. His negotiating appeal to her was, "Come to the table and meet me on this. Let's speak up."

It is possible that Beth had been silenced, which can be a residual effect of childhood sexual abuse. A perpetrator's threats and the survivor's fears silence the survivor regarding the abuse and can spawn a pattern of silence as the survivor's coping mechanism in conflict.

In another couple relationship, Barb's "father–wounds" seemed to be directed at Chad, which resulted in their relational conflict. Chad noted,

> There were strong reactions to just about anything I could do. If I brought her flowers, she could have a very harsh response to me, not the kind of response you would typically get from a wife who gets flowers… If I did something kind when she was at work or something, if I got home and cleaned the kitchen, [she'd say], "It's about time," or it could be some curt response that was meant to wound.

For Dan, the relationship conflict was often due to Nikki's mistrust of him. Dan protested to Nikki,

> *It's like I can't climb this dang mountain fast enough or high enough to get over whatever imaginary barrier you've set, and, damn it, I'm ready to be done with it.*

Dan expanded on his frustration by saying,

> *It was like a game I didn't know the rules to. And frankly, I think she would have been like, "I have no idea what I'm asking you to do, but I just know you're not doing it."*

Dan, along with many other husbands of survivors, described his conflict as "walking on eggshells, not knowing what's going to set her off."

Husbands can feel as though they have to defend themselves for offenses they haven't committed. One husband captured the essence of many husbands whose wives are survivors of childhood sexual abuse.

> *It was like I was in the witness stand, just being drilled. That's what it was like. Oh, I hated it. I tried to be civil. I would try to be patient through it. I'd try to be gentle through it. And, finally, I'd spout, "I'm done. I'm done being examined by you."*

Nelson's wife, Jan, seemed to manage the trauma of her past sexual abuse by attempting to control her environment in the present. If Nelson did not wipe his fingerprints off their stainless steel refrigerator after opening and closing the door, Jan would notice it and note it to Nelson. Being baffled and frustrated by Jan's incessant effort to control, Nelson said with resignation, "When there is no manual on how to handle it, it's hard to understand."

Relationship conflict in marriages involving a survivor of childhood sexual abuse can be fueled by a host of effects from the abuse and the difficulty husbands have in understanding those effects along with how to respond to them. Incidentally, survivors themselves can also have difficulty understanding the effects of their own abuse and how to cope with them.

Relational conflict has various forms and expressions.

**Verbal:** Arguments, sarcasm, shouting, cursing, name–calling, accusations, blaming
**Non–verbal:** Avoidance, the silent treatment, gestures, facial expressions (e.g., rolling one's eyes ), sounds (e.g., grunts and huffs)
**Physical:** Separation, hitting, grabbing, withdrawal (e.g., leaving the room)

## EXPLORING A NEW PERSPECTIVE

Dr. Noelle Wiersma, Dean of the College of Arts and Sciences at Whitworth University has done extensive research in analyzing the communication patterns between survivors of childhood sexual abuse and their partners. Her research identified four domains of relational communication: (a) expressive ability, (b) Expressive Motivation, (c) responsive ability, and (d) responsive motivation.[62] Conflict can occur in each of these domains.

Using Wiersma's four identified domains, let's explore their meaning for you and me as husbands of survivors.

### 1. Expressive Ability

**Expressive ability** refers to the ability of a partner to express what he or she is experiencing as a result of the sexual abuse. This chapter focuses on a husband's ability—or lack thereof—to express what he is experiencing from the effects of his wife's childhood sexual abuse.

My personal experience and that of other husbands whose wives are survivors informs me that we men are often hesitant to express some of our thoughts and feelings to our wives. For some of us, fear hinders our expressive ability. I was fearful that my wife would further distance herself emotionally. Others may fear hostility. The expressive hesitancy on the part of husbands is not limited solely to marriages affected by childhood sexual abuse. However, I know many husbands of sexual abuse survivors bottle–up their feelings and frustrations, feeling unable or unwilling to express their thoughts and feelings.

Patrick and Megan have been married for over twenty–five years. Megan's after effects of abuse were lowered self–esteem, guilt, and depression. I asked Patrick to identify some of his unexpressed thoughts and feelings about his wife and marriage. He answered, "I think some of the thoughts that I didn't express were frustration that she couldn't just put it [the abuse] in the past, forgive herself, and move on. And I guess I never expressed that." Patrick continued, "[I] try not to express conflict. I mean, a lot of people say I avoid conflict, but I try not to express it."

Wiersma noted two obstructions to Expressive Ability. I put those barriers in terms of "I just can't express my thoughts and feelings to her" and "I don't even know my thoughts and feelings to be able to express them."[63] Let's take a closer look at these two obstructions.

### a. I Just Can't Express My Thoughts and Feelings to Her.

Husbands of survivors can experience frustration from any of several hazards in their marriage. These hazards include:

- How he feels so alienated
- Infrequent sexual intimacy
- Her spending habits
- That his wife gets too angry at the kids
- That his wife gets too angry at him
- Her eating habits
- Her compulsive or controlling behaviors

I know that many of you, as husbands, don't need to imagine these things; it's your reality. And you feel paralyzed whenever you consider expressing your thoughts and feelings to your wife. You think to yourself, "It would be helpful to sit down and talk about _____, but I just don't think I can do that now."

I was fearful of bringing up many topics in my marriage. I always panicked when my wife distanced herself from me. But here is something to remember: *she may distance herself, but she comes back.* Unless there are terminal issues in the marriage, she will come back. None of us can live in complete isolation all of the time, even though an occasional day of isolation and serenity sounds appealing. More about this will be stated in the conclusion of this chapter when I talk about the shame–dance.

"I just can't" expresses lack of ability. The second obstruction stems from lack of awareness of oneself.

*b. I Don't Even Know My Thoughts and Feelings…*

I've had a lot of personal experience in this. I had a counselor once ask me how I was doing after a strenuous weekend. I answered how I thought everyone else was doing. So that I would get his point, he rephrased his question and asked, "And how is Bill doing?" There was a moment of long silence as I tried to figure out the answer—more specifically, as I tried to figure out myself.

The first step to being connected with our wives is to be connected with ourselves. Here's a self–check question: *How well do I know what is going on within me so that I can share my soul with me wife?* Here's a helpful exercise. Using SASHET as an acronym, we can identify our feelings by asking, "Am I **S**ad, **A**ngry, **S**cared, **H**appy, **E**xcited, or **T**ender?" The purpose of this self–check is not to find whom I might blame for any negative feelings; rather, it is to take ownership of my feelings.

## 2. Expressive Motivation[64]

While expressive ability refers to our ability to express our thoughts and feelings, **Expressive Motivation** refers to our motivation for saying what we say. Sometimes the deeper motivation is hidden or disguised.

For example, the sexual struggles faced by couples affected by childhood sexual abuse can result in feelings of emasculation in the husband (this is not to minimize the internal struggle encountered by his wife as she contends with memories of sexual invasion). A man's feeling of emasculation is accompanied by a sense of powerlessness. It is not easy for a guy to admit powerlessness, even if he is able to admit it to himself.

When husbands do choose to communicate regarding the infrequency of sexual intimacy, their tone is often that of frustration and anger. The tone of anger disguises his powerlessness and sadness. Anger offers a deluded sense of power and control. The communication becomes messy because it is difficult for our wives, as with anyone, to respond to anger. Therefore, the communication is hindered because of the Expressive Motivation.

In communicating with our wives, if we are not conscious of our *motive*, we will not be clear in our *message*.

### 3. Receptive Ability[65]

Constructive communication between husbands and wives requires intentional and loving expression and receptivity. The third domain in Wiersma's work refers to our level of ability to hear and understand what is expressed by our wives.

Greg Smalley tells the story of the husband and wife whose date night resulted in two vastly different experiences and understandings. Her journal entry at the end of the evening noted the following:

> Tonight, Jim was acting odd. It was our date night, and we went to a nice restaurant for dinner. The ambiance was great. We sat in a nice quiet corner. But unfortunately, our conversation was also quiet; it was even awkward. I asked him what was wrong. He said, "Nothing." I asked him if it was my fault that he was upset. He said he wasn't upset, that it had nothing to do with me, and not to worry about it. On the way home, I told him that I loved him. He smiled slightly and kept driving. When we got home, he just sat there quietly and watched TV. He continued to seem distant and absent. So, I decided that I should just go to bed. He didn't seem to enjoy the evening—or me! It seemed like he was somewhere else. I don't know what to do.

Before Jim went to bed, he entered the following into his journal, "Rough day. Boat wouldn't start, can't figure out why."[66]

Jim exhibited negligible *Receptive Ability* by not receiving his wife's verbal message and emotional plea for connection with him. Preoccupation hinders Receptive Ability.

Wiersma discovered additional ways in which we husbands fail to receive the message from our wives who are survivors of childhood sexual abuse. Our sense of inadequacy to deal with the abuse and its effects can hinder our Receptive Ability.[67] I've interviewed men who wanted their wives to see a counselor not only to get some help but also because they had no idea how to respond to the information about the abuse or their effects from the abuse. Some men don't want any information.

### 4. Receptive Motivation[68]

This fourth domain refers to our motivation for listening. Whereas Receptive Ability refers to our **readiness** for listening, Receptive Motivation refers to our **reason** for listening. Poor Receptive Ability would be when a husband **does not know what to do with** the information about his wife's childhood sexual abuse. Poor Receptive Motivation would be when a husband **does not want to deal with** the information. The refusal to deal with information can be revealed in phrases such as "Can't we just move on?" or "Why can't she just get over this?"

The chart on the next page offers some examples of themes affecting receptivity in partners of survivors and phrases revealing those themes as identified by Wiersma.

Though we do not control our wives' expressive ability or motivation, it is helpful to consider the Receptive Ability of our wives. In *Seven Desires*, Mark and Debbie Laaser offer an insight that applies to how our wives might hear us when we speak.

| Motivational Theme | Examples of Motivational Expression |
|---|---|
| Awareness deemed undesirable | It's probably better that I don't know. |
| Self–deception | Usually, I probably do know what she's thinking. I just tell myself I don't know what she's feeling so I don't feel bad. |
| Projection | I just think about how I would feel about it, how I might deal with it. |
| Failure in perspective taking | I think I'm probably unaware of what [she] feels. |
| Relationship conflict | Sometimes it's made it where I didn't want to be around her as much… I've felt like there's nothing really that I could do to change it, so there are a lot of times when I just do not want to be there at all.[69] |

The Laasers explain how we all develop core beliefs and perceptions. Core beliefs are beliefs we hold about ourselves that are formed in us by the expressions of others and the situations we've experienced. Perceptions are formed and fostered by cultural messages that have been received. To illustrate how our core beliefs and perceptions affect our receptivity, Laasers offer the example of brewing coffee. When you add the water, it runs through the coffee grounds and comes out looking entirely different, dark and brown.[70]

The sexual abuse inflicted on our wives as children functioned as expressions—communications—that formed and fostered in them a set of core beliefs and perceptions. Here's a sampling of some of those core beliefs and perceptions:

- I am dirty.
- It's my fault that something bad happened to me.
- Men cannot be trusted.
- God is neither present nor compassionate.
- All a man wants is my body.
- If people really knew me, they would not like me.

These core beliefs and perceptions are like the coffee grounds. The words you express and the motives behind them may be as pure as the water I pour into my coffee maker. But her core beliefs and perceptions—just as coffee grounds in a brewer—change that message. When you say, "You really look good," she assumes, "You want something". Or when you say, "I'm glad I married you," she thinks, "You really don't know me. I'm dirty."

Difficulty in communication between our wives and us can be traced to a deficiency in one or more of the four domains of communication proposed by Wiersma. Our responsibility as husbands is to examine how and why we are expressing our thoughts and feelings. As receivers of messages from our wives, our responsibility is to assess our level of attentiveness and openness.

**Our responsibility as husbands is to examine
how and why we are expressing our thoughts and feelings.
As receivers of messages from our wives, our responsibility
is to assess our level of attentiveness and openness.**

### ESTABLISHING NEW PATTERNS

There are two extremes in the spectrum of communication for husbands of survivors. I've interacted with husbands who are aggressive communicators with the apparent motivation of fixing their wives or their situation. At the other end of the spectrum are husbands who are "passive" communicators, whose apparent motivation is fear and the attempt to self-protect.

Neither of these forms of communication leads to understanding. The aggressive communicator tends to drive the receiver away. The "passive" communicator is not truly passive because communication still occurs. Granted, words can be the clearest form of communication. But moods and feelings are also communicated through our body language, and sometimes they're very vividly communicated. Misunderstanding is bound to occur when a husband says, "Everything is fine!" with a harsh tone and an angry facial expression.

So, what are some practices and patterns of communication that avoid either of these extremes and whose expressions are informed by the four domains that have been considered? Here are my recommendations that are the outcomes of my own experience and the experiences of others.

### 1. Refuse To Bottle Up Feelings

If we were to take a walk together and a stone got into your shoe, you would soon be taking that shoe off to get rid of the stone. But if we were walking on a beach and sand began accumulating in your shoe, you'd tolerate it for a while. Then, all of a sudden, you'd decide that you've had enough. You'd sit down, take off your shoe, and shake it like crazy to get the sand out.

We do the same when we bottle up feelings. We may think we are able to tolerate the frustration, but suddenly we decide we've had enough, and words of anger and resentment fly out of our mouth just as the sand is shaken out of the shoe. Unfortunately, just like sand flying through the air, our words can sting and be damaging to our relationship. Resentment builds up when we bottle our feelings.

In addition to resentment building up, our bottled-up feelings barricade us from potential individual and relational growth. I learned from Dan and Nikki's experience. Dan's expressive ability developed as healing progressed in their lives. Dan realized that sharing his struggles could become an opportunity for Nikki's development. Referring back to when he bottled up his sexual frustrations, Dan stated, "We found what that did was it denied her the chance to grow through any of it… it never gave her the opportunity to kind of work through the facts." Dan's expressive ability began actually to induce further healing.

## 2. Be An Active Communicator

Here is a fact that has helped me be more communicative: *our wives value the sense of safety.* The threats and trauma imposed on our wives by their perpetrators hurled them into a frightening pit of darkness, despair, loneliness, and shame. They've longed for safety ever since being cast into that pit.

### Our wives value the sense of safety.

I've learned that when I'm not communicating with my wife, she doesn't feel as safe as she deserves to feel. She finds herself in a place where she does not know what is going on; it's a dark and lonely place. My lack of communication leaves her guessing. The dark place is too much like the pit of abuse she was hurled into as a child—a place that left her guessing, where she could not figure out what was going on and what was in the minds of people whose lives were affecting her life and well-being.

In light of this fact—that our wives value a sense of safety—there are two motivating reasons for husbands to be active communicators.

**Other-Focused Motivation:** We can be motivated to communicate out of love for our wives—specifically, out of a heartfelt and selfless desire to ensure that they are safe and that they know they are safe. Out of love, you don't want to leave your wife guessing.

**Common-Sense-Focused Motivation:** We can be motivated to communicate out of our own desire that we not be misunderstood. Our wives can often make inaccurate guesses as to what we are thinking. It is to our advantage to let them know what we are thinking and feeling so that they are not presuming something that is not true. In some cases, if the abuse has interfered with your wife's ability to trust, she will not only *presume* what you are thinking. Your wife might even *construe* what you are thinking. Some survivors are conditioned by their abuse to think the worse. It is common sense that you don't want to leave your wife guessing.

You may argue that your wife needs to grow out of distrust as her default mode of thinking and that she also needs to grow into the awareness that she is safe now that she has been removed from the abuse. Your point is valid. Yes, we do want our wives to grow and heal. At the same time, husbands shoot themselves in the foot if they do not have the emotional intelligence to live in the realm of their wives' reality.

Here's a simple step that we can put into practice: Don't wait for her to have to ask you "What's wrong?" Instead, do your best to identify what it is that has you so preoccupied and share it with your wife. Remember that we men have all our thoughts compartmentalized. And sometimes, like when the boat won't start, we cannot easily get out of that compartment. Share that with your wife and then do all you can to reassure her that you are not upset with her. She may not be completely satisfied, but she'll have a better chance of feeling safe.

Being an active communicator does involve risk because we become more vulnerable as we resist the tendency to bottle up our feelings and actively share our thoughts and feelings. But our vulnerability opens the pathway toward intimacy, knowing and being known.

Refusing to bottle up our thoughts and feelings and becoming active communicators are the first steps to establishing a new pattern. As we establish the pattern of choosing to communicate, we can then consider *how* we shall communicate.

### 3. Consider the What, How, and When of Communication

Before determining what you will say, seek first to understand. What assumptions do you have, and can those assumptions be substantiated? What are your expectations, and what are your wife's expectations? What desire or need are you expressing, and does it in any way conflict with a desire or need of your wife? If so, can you think of a viable solution to the conflicting needs?

How we speak is as important as what we speak. Will our tone of voice engage or enrage? Will our tone convey or cover our true feeling? Will our tone contribute to the building up or tearing down of our wife?

Sense of timing for when we speak is an important component to any productive communication. When is your wife most receptive to conversation? Probably not when she is putting the kids to bed or is late getting off to work. And if she has recently made a further disclosure about her abuse, she may be in a vulnerable time. Therefore, it is not the time to vent a boatload of frustrations. Instead, find a friend or counselor you trust and begin processing your thoughts and identifying your feelings.

I also think it is good to ask ourselves, "Why do I want to say what I want to say? Am I aiming to blame or accuse? Am I in any way reneging on my own responsibility? Am I trying to win or resolve an issue?"

Communication is complex; that's why we say, "Think before you speak."

## 4. Take Inventory of Your Feelings

I have learned that my own fear can get in the way of constructive communication. In the long journey of my wife's healing, there were times when it seemed she was going backward. Sometimes, even new steps of growth can seem like things are going backwards. When things seemed to be going backward, whether it was an actual or only an apparent digression, I would freak out. I was powerless to do anything; and none of us like being powerless.

Since we don't like feeling afraid or powerless, we opt for anger, which gives us the false sense of having control. But speaking in anger to your wife will not resolve anything. She will either fight back or flee, neither of which allows for conversation that promotes understanding and resolution.

When I am more truthful with myself about what I am really feeling, I can then be more truthful with whomever I might be communicating with. The airwaves of both expression and reception are cleared of the static of delusion and self-deception.

## 5. Take Inventory of Your Wife's Feelings

Dr. Daniel Green defines empathy as *the ability to be aware of what it is like to be another person—what their inner experience is like—while being aware simultaneously of one's own inner experience.*[71] It is knowing simultaneously what it is like to be me and what it is like to be you.

> **Empathy is simultaneously knowing what it is like to be me and what it is like to be you.**

Your ability and motivation in both expressing and receiving is governed to a large degree by your level of empathy. In the same way that you must be aware of your desires and feelings rather than bottling them up, you must also be aware of your wife's desires and feelings.

Imagine the husband who is not satisfied with the infrequency of sexual intimacy with his wife, a survivor of childhood sexual abuse. Some of you don't have to imagine this; it's your reality. You probably know by now that making demands about how your sexual drive needs to be satisfied never leads to your wife saying, "Oh, honey, if only you'd let me know sooner."

So what would an empathetic appeal be?

My suggestion towards an empathetic appeal is not a guaranteed cure-all. This book is not about formulas that will win your wife to your point of view. But my suggestion has the likelihood of opening the door for conversation. Here's how you might appeal to your wife:

> We both were made to have sexual intimacy. Sadly, the childhood sexual abuse you had to endure has broken that part for you. I cannot begin to comprehend how difficult that is for you. At the same time, I have not been broken by abuse. So, I long for holding you and you holding me without any shame—nothing between us—to be naked and not ashamed. What do you want me to know so that you can feel safe?

The conversation has started. Where the conversation will go, neither of us can know; that's part of the vulnerability. But you have expressed your need and taken inventory of your wife's need. That's empathy.

## 6. Be Direct Without Being Derogatory

Do not blame, complain, or demand. Notice that blaming can be communicated through statements as well as questions. We blame when we say, "You always…" We also blame through questions like, "Why don't you ever…?"

Statements that begin with. "We never…" typically express a complaint. Instead, it is better to express your need.

Unadulterated motivation in our communication increases as we are willing to be honest, direct, and vulnerable. For example, I might say, "I want you to feel safe, but your safety is compromised if I am not honest. So, I want to be honest, and I am willing to be vulnerable in letting you know my needs. One of those needs is [fill in the blank] and I'd like to talk together about how we can agree so that this need might be met."

Vulnerability is taking the risk of exposing our true motives and desires. We may be turned away. If so, the issue is not within us for we've laid bare our motives before our wives. At the same time, we can know that the more vulnerable we are, the safer our wives can feel, for then nothing in us is disguised and hidden.

## 7. Validate Rather Than Debate

Our wives are not looking for us to fix them. So, take the pressure off yourself. Rather than being fixed, our wives seek to be heard. They have a story—of their abuse—that needs to be told. And if they are going to heal, they need to tell it and we need to receive it—more than just a couple times.

As our wives are able to repeat their stories, they will eventually be able to reveal their emotions. These emotions will be very raw and will include anger, resentment, fear, doubt, and much more. Allow your wife to talk out her emotions rather than trying to talk her out of her emotions.

> **Allow your wife to talk out her emotions rather than trying to talk her out of her emotions.**

## CONCLUSION

Let's return to our diagram from Chapter 8. Intimacy is knowing and being known, requiring the revealing of myself as well as the exploring of the other. The exploration and revelation are mutual and multi–dimensional.

Remember that intimacy deepens as three interactions increase.

**1. Mutuality:** Each individual is engaged in both exploring and revealing.
**2. Totality:** Exploration and revelation occur in all aspects of personhood and experience: past, present, future, intellect, etc.
**3. Vulnerability:** The exploration and revelation reach into deeper layers of the various aspects, requiring loving inquiry in the exploration and trusting vulnerability in the revelation.

Expressive ability and motivation come into play in both the exploring of the other and the revealing of ourselves. In the exploring, we seek to know by the questions we ask. In the revealing, we seek to be known by the thoughts and feelings we share. Motivation is involved in each. Is my motive to know and be known, or is it to prove some point?

My Receptive Ability is enacted when my wife explores my thoughts and feelings, typically in the form of her questions. Am I open to receiving her inquiry, or do I become defensive? Is my motive in receiving to bear with it only so that I can then speak? Or is my motive to listen so that I can then reveal myself?

My Receptive Ability and motivation are also indicated as my wife reveals herself. Am I receptive to her thoughts, needs, and desires, or am I aloof? Is my motive in receiving to gather data so that I can talk her out of her feelings, or is it to grant her the opportunity to talk out her feelings?

Outcomes from the dialogue are not known in advance. That's why we communicate—because of the unknown.

Great expressive and Receptive Ability and the best of motives do not ensure understanding. This chapter's reference to coffee grounds illustrates that each of us has core beliefs about ourselves and perceptions of others that can color and interfere with understanding. Sometimes, we are not even aware of the misunderstanding. Misunderstandings result in a disconnect of intimacy and we enter the shame–dance.

A husband can have one of two common responses when his wife distances herself from him. He might chase after her, which typically prompts her to run faster and further away from him. Or he might withdraw due to a sense of rejection or repulsion. Sadly, in both instances, the distancing increases. Consequently, both husband and wife are engaged in the shame–dance, but no one seems to be in the lead.

Sometimes, it is necessary and best for you to withdraw, but only if it is for the purpose of regrouping and only if it is temporary. Withdrawing becomes destructive when done out of retaliation. But if it is for the purpose of rejuvenation, then it can serve in a constructive way towards reconnection.

Though distancing is an immediate stage in the shame–dance, it need not be the ultimate stance. It is a time to take an inventory of ourselves and of our wife's needs and humbly seek to reestablish understanding through exploring and revealing.

# Chapter 9: Personal Application

1. From this chapter, what steps can you take to develop healthier expressive ability?

2. What have you learned about your motives from this chapter? Think through a recent conflict with your wife. Write down not only what you felt and thought but also why you felt and thought as you did.

3. Let's now consider Receptive Ability and motivation. Neurological evidence points to the fact that trauma alters the brain's normal perceptions for those who were sexually abused as children. The brain's ability to keep the traumatic experience in the past becomes compromised. Therefore, the survivor of childhood sexual abuse is vulnerable to emotionally re-experiencing the past abuse in the present.[72] This means that any acknowledgement of wrong in the present will collide with the trauma of the past.

So how can husbands empathetically respond? Douglas Stone and Sheila Heen offer helpful insights in *Thanks for the Feedback*. They note how easily communication can digress into an "I'm right, you're wrong!" conflict. Their suggestion for an alternative approach includes these steps:

a. Listen for what's right and why she sees it differently. There is neurological evidence that this will take disciplined effort if you feel you are being treated unfairly.

b. Create some inner curiosity—perhaps the message being received isn't entirely unfair. Maybe your wife sees something that you don't or maybe there is something about her view that will be helpful for you to know.

c. Offer evidence that you hear her. Too often, we are like Jim in the opening story. If your wife seems competitive, it may simply be that she is competing for your attention.

d. If you don't agree with the message you are receiving, then add in what's been left out. Stone and Heen state, "You aren't seeking to persuade the giver that you are right. You're not trying to replace their truth with your truth. Instead, you're adding what's 'left out.' And what's most often left out is your data, your interpretations, and your feelings."[73]

Stone and Heen contend that once all the pieces of the puzzle are on the table, you and your wife can begin to see how you perceive things similarly, differently, and why it is so. A successful effort will give evidence of empathy: **your ability to be aware of what it is like to be your wife—what her inner experience is like—while being aware simultaneously of your own inner experience**

For a more in-depth review of this chapter, we have also provided a full, free downloadable "Guide for Application" on our website: www.marriagereconstructionministries.org.
It is our hope that the additional questions in this guide will take you further into potential personal and marital growth.

Chapter Ten

# WHY DOES SHE SEEM TO CHANGE AT THE FLIP OF A SWITCH?

Marriages that include a survivor of childhood sexual abuse can be vulnerable to sudden mood changes and contradictory behaviors. Dawn Scott Jones, in a book that I highly recommend to husbands of childhood sexual abuse survivors, states that,

> Some days she'll want to snuggle close and feel your arms around her, and some days she'll strike out at you in anger and cry, 'Don't touch me.' … Living with a survivor of sexual abuse is a blurry world of uncertainties and double standards.[74]

Another author colorfully stated,

> One minute they [survivors] seem to be cheerful and coping, then, without any apparent reason, they either turn into something resembling a fire–breathing dragon or sink into a bout of depression.[75] Whatever your own experience may be, you can know that you are not alone in dealing with sudden changes.

In my doctoral research, husbands spoke of these sudden changes as occurring at the "drop of a hat" or at the "flip of a switch." Perhaps you can identify with Chad, who spoke of how he was

> *… clueless as to what to do, like on egg shells. I'm walking so gently, I don't want to say anything that will upset her… I don't want to push the wrong buttons. So very, very cautious… I mean, anything could trigger it… it has no rhyme or reason.*

Living with a survivor of childhood sexual abuse is messy because it is filled with unpredictable moods and contradictory behaviors. Before casting blame or categorizing the survivor as being incompatible, husbands need to remember that the inner world of the survivor is filled with memories of unpredictable betrayals, contradictions, and craziness. The unthinkable was their experience.

Dawn Scott Jones advises husbands that in spite of the conflicting emotions that may be pouring out of our wives, "your encouragement and commitment can help her find the courage to discard old habits that protected her."[76]

## EXPLORING A NEW PERSPECTIVE

Many survivors of childhood sexual abuse and its trauma experience a phenomenon known as dissociation. Dissociation is one—but not the only—explanation why some survivors suddenly change. MayoClinic.org states,

> Dissociative disorders are mental disorders that involve experiencing a disconnection and lack of continuity between thoughts, memories, surroundings, actions and identity. People with dissociative disorders escape reality in ways that are involuntary and unhealthy and cause problems with functioning in everyday life.[77]

More simply stated, dissociation is a "mental flight [or detachment] when physical flight is not possible."[78]

Before going further into this topic of dissociation, it is necessary to warn husbands against any attempt to diagnose your wife. There may be other explanations as to why your wife might seem to change at the flip of a switch. At the same time, "Research shows a relationship between dissociation and a history of trauma, most specifically childhood abuse... the highest predictor of dissociative disturbance is childhood sexual abuse."[79] Though not all survivors of childhood sexual abuse suffer from dissociation, it is beneficial to understand this phenomenon since it is not uncommon to survivors of childhood sexual abuse.

I have met husbands of survivors who are unfamiliar with dissociation and are therefore unaware of its possible occurrence in their wives. At the same time,

I've met other husbands whose wives have dissociated. Their familiarity with the phenomenon has contributed to their healthy and empathetic response.

Dissociation functions to shelter the abused child from the pain and memory. A survivor jumps from the intolerable to the tolerable when dissociation occurs. In a very mild sense, most of us dissociate when the dentist is about to extract or drill into a tooth. We dissociate from the dentist chair, mentally placing ourselves on some sunbaked beach or other pleasurable experience.

Dissociation serves as a means of self–protection against the terror or horror of the abuse. When dissociation becomes a practiced coping pattern, it can develop into a disorder known as Dissociative Identity Disorder (DID). With DID, there is the formation of self–generated "alter(s)." A child's *incidental occurrence* of dissociating during abuse can lead to an *intentional experience* of dissociation as an adult through which alter personalities can be created and developed. These alters remain part of one person but assume a distinct identity.

The identification of dissociation and diagnosis of DID is to be determined by a qualified professional counselor. At the same time, I believe it is essential for husbands of survivors to be informed of the phenomenon and equipped to offer an emotionally supportive response. Let's consider a couple examples of how survivors of childhood sexual abuse dissociated. The first example is of Gabbie, who tells her own story.

> *Throughout my life, there were a lot of uncertainties regarding my safety. But no matter how many variations of abuse I experienced, there were a couple of consistencies. Due to the severity and persistence of my father's maltreatment throughout my childhood, my mind began dissociating from my body every time it was being hurt. As the years went on, this coping method grew from a pain response to a constant state of dissociation. I understand how it was effective and helpful when I was being hurt, but now that I am no longer in an environment I need to be afraid of, dissociation has become a disadvantage.*
>
> *For example, as a Little, when the doorbell rang in my home, it meant that some very sickening people were about to enter the already brutal circumstance; it meant I would have to endure a*

*heavier weight of abuse. As a result, that two–note chime I heard every time the door opened evolved into a painstaking trigger that told me I was guaranteed to be hurt.*

*Now, even though I am completely safe from harm, my body's dissociative reaction is still ingrained in me. No matter where I hear a doorbell, I am thrown into flashbacks of past abuse and debilitated by panic. To explain, a couple of these daily situations include I'm watching T.V. and a movie or commercial uses a doorbell sound effect; I am eating dinner with my husband and a package is delivered; I am driving in the car and I hear a doorbell sound on a radio advertisement.*

*The sound of a doorbell chime may seem like a weird thing to cause a crippling fear that collapses my body and shuts down my mind, but it has a real purpose behind it. It stemmed from something that, with time, began to take root and grow. It took countless offenses over the course of many years. I think if you could know just what it represented in my early life, you could see it's a logical trigger.*[80]

You may remember Wes, who used the word "switching" to describe his wife Jyl's experience. Jyl's switching, or dissociation, sometimes followed a disturbing nightmare.

One night, Jyl had a dream that took her back to everything that had happened to her in one incident of her childhood sexual abuse. She awoke disturbed from her dream. Wes, aware of what had happened, got a notebook and instructed her to record what she had just experienced so that she could talk it through with her counselor at her next appointment. Wes described what he then witnessed.

*When I turned and looked at her, that was probably the most shocking experience because I saw her grasping at the pen in a little kid's hand and trying, in little kid's handwriting, to write what was happening to her. It was in the vocabulary of a little kid. It just rocked me because I didn't think that was possible. I turned to her and I saw a look on her face that was the look of childish bewilderment. [I thought], this kid doesn't know how to handle this.*

Accepting and understanding the existence of dissociation as a psychological phenomenon was a learning process for Wes. The existence of dissociation adds to life's uncertainties, affects intimacy, and can be perplexing. When Wes described coming home from work at the end of the day, he said, "I'm going to find either a wife or a kid."

There are many expressions of dissociation among survivors of childhood sexual abuse. Jack's wife sometimes spoke in a childish voice, interjecting childish giggles. Another survivor suddenly charged out of her house and drove away recklessly in her car but had no later recollection of her action.

Dissociation is not always as dramatic as these examples. There are degrees of severity and differences in how it manifests. Here are a few examples, but not proofs, of dissociating experienced by survivors of childhood sexual abuse:

- Not being able to remember segments of the day
- Wishing to be called by another name that is completely different from one's given name or nickname
- Being somewhere and not knowing how you got there
- Covering one's eyes and being unable, not simply unwilling, to speak
- Out–of–body sensation; feeling like you are up in the corner of a room looking down on yourself
- Finding items in your possession that you did not purchase or recall purchasing

Husbands whose wives dissociate can be unfamiliar with the phenomenon and therefore fearful of its expression. A better understanding of how dissociation occurs can reduce that fear.

Tina Zahn experienced dissociative moments common to many survivors of childhood sexual abuse. In *Why I Jumped*, Tina described how her stepfather ordered her to their dark and dingy basement. She recalled how she hated her stepfather's breathing, being held down by him, and the smells that emitted from him. As her stepfather went through his abusive ritual, Tina's thoughts went to her siblings playing outside and the firehouse across the street that represented safety.[81]

The mental transporting of ourselves to another place is a common form of dissociation that can function as a God–given form of self-protection.

Dissociation functions to shelter the abused child from the physical and emotional pain of the traumatic experience.

What, then, is happening within the survivor when dissociation occurs? The BASK model, constructed by B. G. Braun, offers an explanation of dissociation that dispels some of the alarm surrounding its occurrence.

BASK serves as an acronym for the components of our being: *Behavior, Affect, Sensation,* and *Knowledge*. In human experience, especially traumatic experiences, any component can be dissociated from the others. A survivor of childhood sexual abuse may have a sensation that is connected to an event or object yet be disconnected from knowledge of that event. For example, if abuse occurred in a room with a wood–burning stove, the scent–sensation (S) of the burning wood may increase the pulse or anxiety of the survivor when exposed to the sensation in adulthood even though conscious knowledge (K) may be buried.

I advise husbands to pause and reflect when unpredictable and inexplicable responses are received from their wives who are survivors of childhood sexual abuse. When there is an inexplicable response, it is possible that a disconnect might have occurred between any of the components of memory.

The doorbell was a trigger for Gabbie. As with Gabbie, survivors can have a dissociative response to a trigger. For example, a doorbell may sound, or for another survivor it might be someone's touch or hug. As a result, the survivor's blood pressure might escalate, and an escape mode taken without being able to explain the feeling or reaction. These are examples of a disconnect between the Sensation (S) and Behavior (B) from the Knowledge (K) of the event that caused the responses. Any one of the BASK components can be dissociated from the others. In view of Gabbie's example, and as stated by Heather Gingrich, "Once the K component of the BASK model is integrated… it often then feels safer for the client to reexperience the other BASK components."[82]

## ESTABLISHING A NEW PATTERN

A husband's familiarity with the phenomenon of dissociation can contribute to his healthy and empathetic response. Therefore, the first step in establishing a new pattern is to become aware and informed. Hopefully, you know more now than when you began reading this chapter.

Here are some recommendations for a loving and healthy response to a dissociative wife.

### 1. Be calm, compassionate, and confident

If you become agitated, you then add agitation to the immediate situation. Your wife's primary struggle is with her perpetrator, not you. Don't add to her battle. Ask God to calm the storm that you might feel in your own soul.

Allow your wife to speak. You may not have a satisfactory response to her statements and questions, but that's okay. Don't shut her down. It's probable that no one listened to her cry as a child. But you can listen now.

Maintain eye contact. Stay connected with her as best you can. If she becomes aggressive with accusations, do your best to assure her of your love, your commitment to her, and your desire to work through things together. Connect with truth and remain grounded in what you know is real.

Ensure her safety, but don't be controlling. If you attempt to control her, you then step into the place of the perpetrator.

All three C's are necessary: be calm, compassionate, and confident.

### 2. Don't be the therapist

Do not say, "I think this is happening because [fill in the blank]" or "Is this the [alter name or title] personality?"

Even if you are convinced your wife had a dissociative episode, she may not be aware of it, nor is it your role to convince her of it. Keep in mind that her alter personality functioned to protect her conscious state. Only after effective counseling and some successful integration will your wife be able to recognize the occurrence of a dissociative incident.

### 3. Love the whole person

A past school of thought proposed relating to the dissociative individual on the same level as their alter personality. For example, if your wife was in a dissociative state as an eight-year-old, then you would relate to the alter as you would to any eight-year-old. In recent decades, this methodology has been discouraged. The focus has shifted toward integration of the alter personalities.

When dissociation occurs, husbands are to show respect. Never belittle or ridicule. Love her for all that she is.

No one is the same all the time. For example, our moods can shift from one day to the next and from one moment to the next. We are grateful for those who love us whether we are in a good mood or in a funk. Our wives, made in the image of God, are worthy of the same consistent love no matter what their mood or condition.

### 4. Forty-eight hours

After a significant dissociative occurrence, it takes time for the survivor to get back into a more balanced state. It can take up to forty-eight hours. As my wife's former counselor would always tell me, "Be patient!" I got tired of hearing it, but he was right.

### 5. Take inventory and responsibility for your own feelings

When my wife has had a dissociative experience, I typically feel lonely. My counselor has reminded me that *loneliness is a longing for someone to return.* With dissociation, we do wait for our wives to return psychologically. That means it's time again for me to be patient until she does return to connect.

Loneliness is a common experience for husbands of survivors. It is necessary to have close relationships with other men. It is also necessary to have a counselor with whom we can process our fears and loneliness.

### 6. Remember that your children are in the house

If you have children living at home, remember that they are very much connected and in tune with their mom, your wife. Just because they may not be saying anything does not mean that they are not being affected. Developmentally, your children may not have the words or concepts by which to communicate their well-being or lack thereof.

Again, it is necessary to discuss your situation with a qualified counselor who can advise you regarding the best course of action for your children. Be sure that your counselor and that your wife's counselor has experience in working with survivors who dissociate.

## CONCLUSION

Social relationship conflict can be a problematic issue in marriages affected by a spouse's childhood sexual abuse. Husbands of survivors know that the memory of their wife's childhood trauma can be triggered when any of the five senses are stimulated by any environment condition or relational interactions that accompanied their trauma decades earlier.

The trigger can rouse an unpredictable response with unexpected intensity.

Our olfactory center—our sense of smell—has a powerful ability to trigger memory. It's perhaps the most powerful of our senses to do so. For example, a young or older woman may wonder why the fragrance of spring blossoms triggers for her an unnatural response—one contrary to its beauty. She may wonder why, rather than desiring a deeper breath of the fragrance, she feels some nausea at the slightest whiff. What if that woman as a young girl, was sexually abused in a room while the fragrance of spring blossoms was wafting through an open window? Wouldn't the nausea then make sense? Wouldn't her unnatural response actually begin to become a rational response? However, if her husband doesn't empathetically understand the fragrance's link to the past, he may deem her to be irrational.

The survivor's triggered memory of her past trauma can elicit a response in the form of words, gestures, facial expressions, or silence. For some, the event triggers a disengagement from the present: dissociation.

Dr. Daniel Green, Clinical Director at New Life Resources in Waukesha, Wisconsin, has reminded me that *dissociation is coping with overwhelming material.* In the case of childhood sexual abuse, dissociation is a God–given gift to deal with sinful atrocities done against our wives.

Wes, the husband of a survivor, proposed that though God allows evil such as childhood sexual abuse to occur, He ministers to the child through the mechanism of dissociation. Wes recounted the sexual abuse inflicted on one of his wife's sisters, who, during the act of abuse, appeared to dissociate. She saw herself up in the corner of the room in Jesus' hands, and Jesus was crying, and His tears were washing all the filth of the abuse off of her.

I love the conclusion Wes drew from this incident. He said,

*Isn't that just like the God we have to provide a mechanism for little kids to escape the awfulness of what they're going through? God is not violating the chance for everyone to do good or evil. And there was a guy [the perpetrator] doing evil. But God isn't going to intervene and say, "That guy can't do evil." No, that guy can still do evil. But He, our loving God, provides a mechanism for little kids to escape the awful reality of where they are and still stay sane.*

Integration can occur with good counseling. The process of integration will require our patience as husbands and unconditional support through the counseling process.

# Chapter 10: Personal Application

1. Write down how your wife's inner world as a child was filled with memories of unpredictable betrayals, contradictions, and craziness.

2. How might your wife's childhood experience of unpredictable betrayals, contradictions, and craziness shed light on her current behavior and responses?

3. Jot down three things you learned or were reminded about from this chapter regarding dissociation.

4. Review the six recommendations listed in the section "Establishing New Patterns." For each one, write down one or two actions you can take in order for you to develop further in offering a loving and healthy response to your wife.

For a more in-depth review of this chapter, we have also provided a full, free downloadable "Guide for Application" on our website: www.marriagereconstructionministries.org.
It is our hope that the additional questions in this guide will take you further into potential personal and marital growth.

# CONCLUSION

A few months ago, while I was in the process of writing this book, I came across a document stored in my computer that I was surprised to find. The document contained a prayer to God from fourteen years ago. "Prayer" seems rather bland. It was a desperate plea.

Perhaps you will be able to identify with the sense of desperation in this plea to God. I'm guessing you will.

Here it is:

*September 8, 2004*

*Lord,*

*I hurt so bad. I am so despairing over Pamela's condition this week. The contrast of disposition rips at my soul. I look back to intimate times, whether talking at one of our favorite cafes or riding on the motorcycle this summer and feel like I've lost my love. I realize that the pain I feel for her is nothing compared to the pain she feels herself. But I don't know what to do. I cannot fix it by attempting to cheer her up. I become immobilized in the pain myself. How is a loving husband to help carry his wife's burden yet function when the pain is so deep? How do I keep from being bogged down in the pain without just detaching emotionally altogether?*

*I know you are with me, yet I feel so left alone.*
*I know you are triumphant, yet I realize that doesn't mean things go my way.*
*I know you invite us to ask, yet I cannot demand.*

*I do ask that—*
- *You would in some way bring comfort and hope to Pamela.*
- *You would give her courage to love again.*
- *You would bless her as Your precious daughter.*
- *You would strengthen her to face the reality of the abuse and the grace to forgive the abuser.*
- *You would guard her and keep her for Your ongoing healing.*
- *You would heal my family.*
- *You would give me grace, comfort, courage, and hope.*

*I do know that—*
- *Your love for us is infinitely greater than any love we could claim to have for others*
- *You are pure and perfect*
- *You claim us as your own children*
- *You are good*
- *You are triumphant*

*I look back on how things have changed over the past month. We've never gone deeper in our conversations with each other than we did a month ago. We thought and felt as one. We also knew that whatever You had ahead for us, You were going to take us deeper into Yourself. Lord, if that is what this is about, I accept it. But please do not hide from us. May shame not be brought to Your name. I lay this out before You, not by any merit of my own. I present this letter to You through the name of Your Son, Jesus Christ.*

*Bill*

The amazing thing to me is that I have no recollection of the events surrounding this prayer nor of having recorded the prayer. And though I can believe that I felt as distraught as the tone of the prayer suggests, I have a difficult time connecting with that feeling now.

My inability to connect now with the desperate feelings I had then is due to the fact that healing can occur in our lives and marriages and that there is hope. I know that there are other husbands of survivors who have also experienced this healing, as have their wives.

Sadly, I realize that not every marriage heals. I assume you, as a husband, want healing. Otherwise, you wouldn't have bothered reading this book. But not every survivor heals sufficiently for a healthy marriage. Some do not realize their unhealthy condition and others don't want to face the pain in order to progress toward healing. I grieve for you and pray that God will in some way grant you emotional health and spiritual strength. God is able to redeem the worst of circumstances.

For those who have experienced healing in your life and marriage, you know that the process of healing is ongoing. Just as there are physical wounds and scars, there are also emotional wounds and scars. And just as a physical wound can be irritated by its being rubbed or scratched, so also emotional wounds can be irritated. These irritations can be the words, smells, sounds, sights, and other triggers noted in this book.

My wife and I were recently at an open mic night at a café in a distant city. One of the performers was a woman who presented her tragic story via a lyrical reading. I've never understood poetic styling, so I was slow to grasp what she was communicating. My gut sensed that it was about being raped. I looked over at my wife who connects intimately with lyrical form and was connecting empathetically with the presenter. It was about rape. The reading took my wife into darkness and anxiousness.

As we walked back towards our hotel, I felt sad for the woman, but I was able to set her feelings and even my feelings behind me. Not so for my wife. Her present had once again been harshly invaded by her past. It wasn't just about the woman's experience, it was about my wife's. She not only knew the feelings expressed by the woman, she felt her actual feelings. My wife's well-healed wounds had been poked and jabbed.

In situations like the one I've just described, recovery for our wives is not overnight. It can take days and sometimes weeks.

Some of our own fears as husbands can resurface when we observe our wives struggling. In spite of the fact that I know the setbacks are temporary and that the cloud will lift as my wife works through the invasion of the past, I still have moments of being confused and scared.

There are countless ways that the past invades. Wes, who was cited multiple times in this book, gave me a call this morning. We haven't talked for over a year. But he and his wife are currently experiencing the present invasion of the past trauma as they have had to re-engage with her perpetrator. I will not speak for them, but if I was in their shoes, I'd be dealing with a lot of horror and anger.

When the painful past once again invades our peaceful present, it is time to revisit the perspectives and patterns outlined in this book. Once again, as noted in the introduction of this book, it is time to learn more about God—His love and His presence—and more about ourselves as we journey toward greater individual and marital health. As we go deeper into the certainty of truth, we will advance further into the experience of freedom.

# ABOUT THE AUTHOR

Dr. Bill Ronzheimer is President of Marriage Reconstruction Ministries, Inc. (MRM) whose mission is to help men and women rebuild marriages affected by a wife's childhood sexual abuse. Prior to launching MRM in 2016, Bill served as Lead Pastor of Alliance Bible Church in Mequon, Wisconsin for 39 years. His marriage to a survivor of childhood sexual abuse, years of experience as a pastor to healthy and hurting families, and doctoral research of husbands married to survivors of sexual abuse have given him a deep and broad foundation for his current work.

Bill received his doctorate in 2013 from Oxford Graduate School (Dayton, TN). During this time, he was the recipient of the Grail Award for Excellence in Research for his work.

Bill offers one-on-one care and support to husbands of survivors and writes blogs and articles addressing issues encountered by both survivors of sexual abuse and their spouses. He and his wife Pamela openly share their own journey and convey principles that are spiritually and psychologically sound. They speak at conferences and seminars, universities, and churches.

Bill and Pamela have been married for over 46 years. They live in the Twin Cities area of Minnesota, close to their two married daughters and three grandchildren.

To learn more: marriagereconstructionministries.org

# APPENDIX A

**DSM–5 CRITERION FOR PTSD**

Diagnostic criteria for 309.81 Posttraumatic Stress Disorder

A. Exposure to actual or threatened death, serious injury, or sexual violence in one (or more) of the following ways:
   1. Directly experiencing the traumatic event(s).
   2. Witnessing, in person, the event(s) as it occurred to others.
   3. Learning that the traumatic event(s) occurred to a close family member or close friend. In cases of actual or threatened death of a family member or friend, the event(s) must have been violent or accidental.
   4. Experiencing repeated or extreme exposure to aversive details or the traumatic event(s) (e.g., first responders collecting human remains; police officers repeatedly exposed to details of child abuse).
   **Note:** Criterion A4 does not apply to exposure through electronic media, television, movies, or pictures, unless this exposure is work related.

B. Presence of one (or more) of the following intrusion symptoms associated with the traumatic event(s), beginning after the traumatic event(s) occurred:
   1. Recurrent, involuntary, and intrusive distressing memories of the traumatic event(s).
   **Note:** In children older than 6 years, repetitive play may occur in which themes or aspects of the traumatic event(s) are expressed.
   2. Recurrent distressing dreams in which the content and/or effect of the dream are related to the traumatic event(s).
   **Note:** In children, there may be frightening dreams without recognizable content.
   3. Dissociative reactions (e.g., flashbacks) in which the individual feels or acts as if the traumatic event(s) were recurring. (Such reactions may occur on a continuum, with the most extreme  expression being a complete loss of awareness of present surroundings.)

**Note:** In children, trauma–specific reenactment may occur in play.

4. Intense or prolonged psychological distress at exposure of internal or external cues that symbolize or resemble an aspect of the traumatic event(s).

5. Marked physiological reactions to internal or external cues that symbolize or resemble an aspect of the traumatic event(s).

C. Persistent avoidance of stimuli associated with the traumatic event(s), beginning after the traumatic event(s) occurred, as evidenced by one or both of the following:

1. Avoidance of or efforts to avoid distressing memories, thoughts, or feelings about or closely associated with the traumatic event(s).

2. Avoidance of or efforts to avoid external reminders (people, places, conversations, activities, objects, situations) that arouse distressing memories, thoughts, or feelings about or closely associated with the traumatic event(s).

D. Negative avoidance in cognitions and mood associated with the traumatic event(s), beginning or worsening after the traumatic event(s) occurred, as evidenced by two (or more) of the following:

1. Inability to remember an important aspect of the traumatic event(s) (typically due to dissociative amnesia and not to other factors such as head injury, alcohol, or drugs).

2. Persistent and exaggerated negative beliefs or expectations about oneself, others, or the world (e.g., I am bad, No one can be trusted, The world is completely dangerous, My whole nervous system is permanently ruined).

3. Persistent, distorted cognitions about the cause or consequences of the traumatic event(s) that lead the individual to blame himself/ herself or others.

4. Persistent negative emotional state (e.g., fear, horror, anger, guilt, or shame).

5. Markedly diminished interest or participation in significant activities.

6. Feelings of detachment or estrangement from others.

7. Persistent inability to experience positive emotions (e.g., inability to experience happiness, satisfaction, or loving feelings).

E. Marked alterations in arousal and reactivity associated with the traumatic event(s), beginning or worsening after the traumatic event(s) occurred, as evidenced by two (or more) of the following:

1. Irritable behavior and angry outburst (with little or no provocation) typically expressed as verbal or physical aggression toward people or objects.
2. Reckless or self–destructive behavior.
3. Hypervigilance.
4. Exaggerated startle response.
5. Problems with concentration.
6. Sleep disturbance (e.g., difficulty falling or staying asleep or restless sleep).

F. Duration of the disturbance (Criteria B, C, D, and E) is more than 1 months.

G. The disturbance causes clinically significant distress or impairment in social, occupational, or other important areas of functioning.

H. The disturbance is not attributable to the physiological effects of a substance (e.g., medication, alcohol) or another medical condition.[83]

# REFERENCES

1. Davis, Laura, Allies in Healing: When the Person You Love Was Sexually Abused as a Child (New York: HarperCollins, 1991), 143.

2. Jeff Feldhahn and Shaunti Feldhahn, For Men Only: A Straightforward Guide to the Inner Lives of Women (Colorado Springs, CO: Multnomah Books, 2013), 42.

3. Feldhahn and Feldhahn, For Men Only, 45.

4. Kay Yerkovich and Milan Yerkovich, How We Love: Discover Your Love Style, Enhance Your Marriage (Colorado Springs, CO: Waterbrook Press, 2006), 49.

5. Daniel Green and Russ Pope, Connection and Healing: A 200–Day Journey into Recovery (Carefree, AZ: Gentle Path Press, 2010), 44.

6. Green and Pope, Connection and Healing, 406–409.

7. Green and Pope, Connection and Healing, 409.

8. Ronzheimer, William C., Husbands Speak: The Perceived Impact of a Wife's Childhood Sexual Abuse on a Marriage Relationship (PhD diss., Oxford Graduate School at Dayton, TN, 2013), 152–60.

9. Daniel Green, Counseling Session at New Life Resources Waukesha, WI, 2015.

10. Gershen Kaufman, PhD., The Psychology of Shame: Theory and Treatment of Shame–Based Syndromes (New York: Springer Publishing, 1989), 25.

11. Carolynn P. Maltas, and Joseph Shay, "Trauma Contagion in Partners of Survivors of Childhood Sexual Abuse," American Journal of Orthopsychiatry 65, no. 4 (1995): 529–39.

12. Maltas and Shay, Trauma Contagion, 533.

13. Maltas and Shay, Trauma Contagion, 532.

14. Patrick J. Carnes, PhD., Trauma Bonds (Louisville, KY: Healing Tree), https://healingtreenonprofit.org/wp–content/uploads/2016/01/Trauma–Bonds–by–Patrick–Carnes–1.pdf.

15. Pauline Boss, Ambiguous Loss: Learning to Live with Unresolved Grief (Cambridge, MA: Harvard University Press, 1999).

16. John W. James and Russell Friedman, The Grief Recovery Handbook (New York: HarperCollins, 2009), 26–36.

17. Elisabeth KRoss, On Death and Dying (New York: Scribner Publishing, 1969).

18. John Townsend, Hiding from Love: How to Change the Withdrawal Patterns That Isolate and Imprison You (Grand Rapids, MI: Zondervan Publishing House, 1996), 100.

19. Brennan Manning, Abba's Child: The Cry of the Heart for Intimate Belonging (Colorado Springs, CO: NavPress), 16.

20. E. R. C. Walker, Thomas B. Holman and Dean M. Busby, Childhood Sexual Abuse, Other Childhood Factors, and Pathways to Survivors' Adult Relationship Quality, Journal of Family Violence 24 (2009): 397–406.

21. John Courtright and Sid Rogers, What to Do When You Find Out... Your Wife Was Sexually Abused (Grand Rapids, MI: Zondervan Publishing House, 1994), 52–58.

22. James G. Jensen, Step Two: A Promise of Hope, Alcoholics Anonymous (Hazelden, 1992), 10.

23. David Brooks, The Road to Character (New York, NY: Random House, 2015), 22.

24. Manning, Abba's Child, 102.

25. Kirk Livingston, Listen Talk: Is Conversation an Act of God? (Bloomington, IN: IUniverse, 2015), 56.

26. Katherine Ketcham and Ernest Kurtz, The Spirituality of Imperfection: Storytelling and the Search for Meaning (New York: Bantam Books, 1992), 118.

27. Ketcham and Kurtz, The Spirituality of Imperfection, 118.

28. Archibald D. Hart, Regeneration, Deliverance, and Therapy? Leadership Journal 12 (Summer 1991): 72–81.

29. Secondary Survivor refers to those in close enough relationship with a primary survivorsuch as a survivor of childhood sexual abuse that they too experience a degree of traumatic effect from the trauma experience by the primary survivor.

30. Robert A. Ferguson and Rory Remer, Becoming a Secondary Survivor of Sexual Assault, Journal of Counseling and Development 73, no. 4 (March 1995): 407–413. The headings for each marker and the general descriptions of each are drawn directly from Remer and Ferguson. The examples are drawn from my personal research.

31. See Chapter 10 for a more expanded explanation of this phenomenon.

32. Wading, The Free Dictionary of the English Language. 5th ed. (2011), accessed June 2, 2018, https://www.thefreedictionary.com/wading

33. Sharon E. Cheston, As You and the Abused Person Journey Together (New York: Paulist Press, 1994), 61.

34. Green and Pope, Connection and Healing, 44.

35. Les Sellnow, Foal Imprinting – The Horse, The Horse, September 30, 2017, accessed June 2, 2018, http://www.thehorse.com/articles/10405/foal–imprinting.

36. David W. Foy, Ned Rodriguez, Anderson Rowan, and Susan Ryan, Posttraumatic Stress Disorder in a Clinical Sample of Adult Survivors of Childhood Sexual Abuse, Child Abuse and Neglect 20, no. 10 (1996): 943–952. In one study, 117 help–seeking adult survivors of CSA were assessed with a research purpose of exploring the relationship between the CSA and PTSD. Results indicated that 72% of the sample met full DSM–III–R criteria for PTSD at the time of the study and 14% met the criteria for partial PTSD. It was also reported that 86% met full DSM–III–R criteria for PTSD at some point during their lives and 6% met the criteria for partial PTSD.

37. Heather Davediuk Gingrich, Restoring the Shattered Self: A Christian Counselor's Guide to Complex Trauma (Downers Grove, IL: IVP Academic, 2013).

38. Diagnostic and Statistical Manual of Mental Disorders 5th Edition (Arlington, VA: American Psychiatric Publishing, 2013).

39. S.R. Gold, Brief Research Report: History of Child Sexual Abuse and Adult Sexual Fantasies, Violence and Victims 6, no. 1 (1991): 75–82

40. Stacie E. Putman, The Monsters in My Head: Posttraumatic Stress Disorder and the Child Survivor of Sexual Abuse, Journal of Counseling and Development 87, no. 1 (Winter 2009): 80–89.

41. Susan Johnson and Heather B. MacIntosh, Emotionally Focused Therapy for Couples and Childhood Sexual Abuse Survivors, Journal of Marital and Family Therapy 34, no. 3 (2008): 298–315.

42. Susan M. Johnson and Lyn Williams–Keeler, Creating Healing Relationships for Couples Dealing with Trauma: The Use of Emotionally Focused Marital Therapy, Journal of Marital and Family Therapy 24, no. 1 (January 1998): 25–40.

43. Maltas and Shay, Trauma Contagion, 529–539.

44. Sarah Boyle and Madge Bray, Sexual Abuse – The Child's Voice: Poppies on the Rubbish Heap (London: Jessica Kingsley Publishers, 1997): 195.

45. Clark E. Barshinger, Lojan E. LA Rowe, and Andres T. Tapia, Haunted Marriage: Overcoming the Ghosts of Your Spouse's Childhood Abuse (Downers Grove, IL: InterVarsity Press, 1995): 11.

46. Frederick Buechner, Wishful Thinking: A Theological ABC (New York: Harper & Row, 1973): 2.

47. Roy Lloyd and Robert Enright PhD., The Science of Forgiveness, The Huffington Post, May 25, 2011, https://www.huffingtonpost.com/roy–lloyd/the–science–of–forgivenes_b_613138.html.

48. Robert D. Enright, PhD., Forgiveness is a Choice: A Step–by–Step Process for Resolving Anger and Restoring Hope (Washington, DC: American Psychological Association, 2001).

49. Greg Boyd, sermon delivered at Woodland Hills Church, St. Paul, MN, March 23, 2012. These are my personal notes from listening to Greg's sermon.

50. Brett Cassidy, The Things Women Do to Emasculate Men, AskMen, November 28, 2017, https://au.askmen.com/top_10/dating/things–women–do–to–emasculate–men_7.html.

51. Maltas and Shay, Trauma Contagion, 529–539.

52. Manning, Abba's child, 165.

53. Melody Beattie, Codependent No More: How to Stop Controlling Others and Start Caring for Yourself (Center City, MN: Hazelden, 1986).

54. Alasdair Groves, Exposing the Lies of Pornography and Counseling the Men Who Believe Them, The Journal of Biblical Counseling 27, no. 1 (2013): 7–25.

55. Groves, Exposing the Lies, 12.

56. Joe Carter, 9 Things You Should Know About Pornography and the Brain, The Gospel Coalition (TGC), October 31, 2017, https://www.thegospelcoalition.org/article/9-things-you-should-know-about-pornography-and-the-brain/. [57] Elisabeth O. Burgess and Denise A. Donnell, The Decision to Remain in an Involuntary Celibate Relationship, Journal of Marriage and Family 70, no. 2 (May, 2008): 519–535.

58. David C. Hoover and Alex W. Kwee, Theologically-Informed Education about Masterbation: A Male Sexual Health Perspective, Journal of Psychology and Theology 36, no. 4 (2008): 258–269.

59. Debra Laaser and Mark Laaser, Seven Desires: Looking Past What Separates Us to Learn What Connects Us (Grand Rapids, MI: Zondervan, 2013).

60. Robert Barry Levine, When You Are the Partner of a Rape or Incest Survivor: A Workbook for You (San Jose, CA: Resource Publications, 1996), 79.

61. Green and Pope, Connection and Healing, 412–413.

62. Noelle S. Wiersma, Partner Awareness Regarding the Adult Sequelae of Childhood Sexual Abuse for Primary and Secondary Survivors, Journal of Marital and Family Therapy 29, no. 2 (May 2003): 151–164. Available for purchase at: http://onlinelibrary.wiley.com/doi/10.1111/j.17520606.2003.tb01197.x/abstract

63. Wiersma, Partner Awareness, 154–155.

64. Wiersma, Partner Awareness, 155.

65. Wiersma, Partner Awareness, 159.

66. Greg Smalley, Dr., Fight Your Way to a Better Marriage: How Healthy Conflict Can Take You to Deeper Levels of Intimacy (New York: Howard Books, 2013), 88.

67. Wiersma, Partner Awareness, 159.

68. Wiersma, Partner Awareness, 159.

69. Wiersma, Partner Awareness, 159–161.

70. Laaser and Laaser, Seven Desires, 82.

71. Green, Counseling Session.

72. Abby Levenkron and Steven Levenkron, Stolen Tomorrows: Understanding and Treating Women's Childhood Sexual Abuse (New York: W. W. Norton & Company, 2007), 154. [73] Sheila Heen and Douglas Stone, Thanks for the Feedback: The Science and Art of Receiving Feedback Well (New York: Penguin Books, 2014), 234–242.

74. Dawn Scott Jones, When a Woman You Love Was Abused: A Husband's Guide to Helping Her Overcome Childhood Sexual Molestation (Grand Rapids, MI: Kregel Publications, 2012), 14–15.

75. Robert Cardwell, Through it Together: Help and Advice for Partners of Survivors of Child Abuse (London: Minerva, 1998), 26.

76. Jones, Thanks for the Feedback, 13.

77. Dissociative Disorders, Mayo Clinic, November 17, 2017, accessed July 30, 2018, https://www.mayoclinic.org/diseases-conditions/dissociative-disorders/symptoms-causes/syc-20355215.

78. Christiane Sanderson, Counseling Adult Survivors of Child Sexual Abuse. 3rd ed. (London: Jessica Kingsley, 2006), 187.

79. Sanderson, Counseling, 183.

80. Gabbie (Pseudonym), Submitted quote by survivor and shared with permission, September 26, 2017.

81. Tina Zahn and Wanda Dyson, Why I Jumped: My True Story of Postpartum Depression, Dramatic Rescue & Return to Hope (Grand Rapids, MI: Revell, 2006), 18–20.

82. Gingrich, Restoring the Shattered Self, 111.

83. Diagnostic and Statistical Manual of Mental Disorders. 5th ed. (Washington, DC: American Psychiatric Publishing, 2013), 271–272.

Made in United States
Troutdale, OR
01/03/2024